HOUSTON PUBLIC LIBRARY
HOUSTON, TEXAS
GIFT OF

MR. E. T. KELLEY

S0-ACB-314

RIPLEY,

THE MODERN
MARCO POLO

BOOKS BY BOB CONSIDINE

MacArthur the Magnificent
30 Seconds over Tokyo (with Captain Ted Lawson)
Where's Sammy? (with Sammy Schulman)
General Wainwright's Story (with Jonathan Wainwright)
The Babe Ruth Story (with Babe Ruth)
The Rape of Poland (with Stanislaw Mikolajczyk)
Where I Stand (with Harold Stassen)
The Maryknoll Story
Innocents at Home
Man Against Fire
Dempsey (with Bill Slocum)
Christmas Stocking
Khrushchev and the Russian Challenge (with W. R.
Hearst, Jr., and Frank Conniff)
The Men Who Robbed Brink's (with Specs O'Keefe)
It's the Irish

RIPLEY,

THE MODERN
MARCO POLO

BY BOB CONSIDINE

B
R48c

DOUBLEDAY & COMPANY, INC.

GARDEN CITY, NEW YORK

RO1 0327 3408

Copyright © 1961 by Robert Considine
All Rights Reserved
Printed in the United States of America

64- 3031

To DOUG STORER
The man Ripley said was the first person
who believed in BELIEVE IT OR NOT

An Author's Note:

IT borders on the superfluous to report that this book about Bob Ripley is not the work of one man, as its glowing by-line might lead the unwary to believe. Many gave a hand to this attempt to paint, with the sternly regimented English alphabet, a recognizable likeness of a curious genius who lived the life of a Roman candle. Without those helping hands this land would still be plagued with an increasingly virulent cliché: "Why doesn't somebody write a book about Bob Ripley?"

Ripley's friends, some of them from the earliest days of his still incredible climb in cartooning, are herewith warmly thanked for their memories. They encompass a range of professions and interests which betokens Ripley's own virtuosity. The roll call shows Senator Barry Goldwater, Bugs Baer, Pulitzer Prize-winning Rube Goldberg, Ross Allen, Vyvyan Donner, Representative Edwin Dooley, Ed Dunham, Bill Dunn, Jack Egan, Carol Ennis, Dick Hyman, Bradley Kelly, Red Lobdell, Frank Mack, Frank Maxwell, Don McClure, Harry Ommerle, Norbert Pearlroth, Samuel Pryor, Mrs. B. A. Rolfe, Max Schuster, Louis Sobol, Douglas and Hazel Storer, Robert Taplinger, Paul Terry, Lowell Thomas, Ilya Tolstoy, Kenneth Webb, Joe Willicombe, Jimmy and Marjorie Young, and many others.

Their solid anecdotes and the bits and fragments of additional reminiscences were sifted, checked, and put in order by two gifted associates: Tom Meany, the wittiest baseball historian of them all; and Milton Kaplan, editor of Hearst Headline Service. To Messrs. M. and K., therefore, a deep bow.

King Features Syndicate has done amazing jobs of keeping life in features whose creators passed on. "Believe It or Not" stands at the head of this list of daily resuscitations. As Rip's masterful pen fell from his hand it was figuratively and all but literally caught in mid-air by Paul Frehm, an artist of rare skill, verve, and strength who had been doing Ripley's "outside" jobs—notably the Borg-Warner advertisements—for several years. It was but a short leap from there to Ripley's daily cartoon. The style was identical in its impact, the taste just as infallible, the sense of awe just as keen. The feature continues to attract new clients.

It is a poignant tribute to his timelessness that several hundred letters a week are sent either to Ripley personally or to the feature that will always bear his bold posthumous signature. School children confronted by composition chores write in and ask for his "files" on, let us say, Abraham Lincoln. Pet fanciers swamp him with news of deeds, heroic or eccentric, performed by their creatures. Diet-conscious readers bombarded the Ripley office with cries for more details on the meal program of one Mrs. Celesta Geyer of Long Beach, California, who lost 435 pounds in 14 months (she trimmed down from a voluptuous 555 pounds). An Ecuadorian recently shipped a shrunken head to "Ripley," with a covering note reading, "Please take good care of this. I think it is one of my relatives."

Ripley might have proved it was.

BOB CONSIDINE

RIPLEY,

THE MODERN
MARCO POLO

CHAPTER I

Ripley's Greatest Oddity

IT was late spring 1929, and into the lobby of the New York Athletic Club strode a tall, trim, determined-looking man in his mid-thirties. As he approached the reception desk, he called out, "Where can I find Bob Ripley?" If his voice had not carried so well, and carried with it such a ring of authority, Joseph V. Connolly might have found Ripley not fifty feet away, emerging from an elevator. But Ripley, at the time threatened with a breach-of-promise suit, mistook the stern-looking Connolly for a process server and ducked out a side door and into the vastness of Central Park. There he spent the rest of the day, procrastinating, until Connolly was able to get into Ripley's room and trap him a few days later, a meeting that would alter Ripley's life in a manner beyond his wildest dreams and set in motion a personal drama more bizarre than anything he ever portrayed in his "Believe It or Not" cartoon.

Connolly, one of the great editors of all time, was head of King Features Syndicate, by far the world's largest purveyor of comic strips, columns, and assorted newspaper features. He had a prolific imagination and relentless drive. He had the vast wealth and other resources of the Hearst newspaper empire behind him. And before him he had a two-word telegram from William Randolph Hearst, Sr., then at the very peak of his power and majesty. It said simply: SIGN RIPLEY.

One of the special skills for which Hearst editors were unusually well paid was the knack of deciphering and executing terse and peremptory telegrams and cables from "The Chief." Some of the decoding operations set off were agonizing—once King Features executives received from Bad Nauheim, Germany, where Hearst was vacationing, a two-worder reading: GET ANDERSON; only after the most painstaking examination of periodicals, feature directories, and their memories did the KFS men decide—correctly, as it turned out—that WRH wanted Carl Henry Anderson, a cartoonist then employed on the *Saturday Evening Post*. There were, of course, bound to be breakdowns in communication of this nature: a two-word cable from Paris prompted the dramatic promotion to head of one Hearst subsidiary for a young underling whose chief asset was a last name shared with the man Hearst really wanted. There was no doubt in Connolly's mind whom Hearst was referring to, however, when he directed him to SIGN RIPLEY.

King was then only one of a number of syndicates trying to hire Ripley. For his career and fortunes had just had a notable boost through the efforts of another persuasive and persistent editor, Max Schuster, of Simon and Schuster. Intrigued by the Ripley "Believe It or Not" cartoons appearing at the time in the New York *Post*, Schuster spent nearly four years encouraging Ripley to compile some of his cartoons into a book. For a long time Ripley demurred, saying, "I'm just a two-cent man"—that was the price of newspapers in those days. Schuster cajoled, promised, even dug up curiosa for Ripley, and the reluctant author finally got some two hundred of his cartoons between hard covers.

Schuster didn't stop there. He sent one of the first copies out of the bindery to Hearst, because he was certain that the great publisher's widely heralded appreciation of the unusual would lead him to approve Ripley's approach to the odd and arresting detail—and that in turn would result in promotion of the book through the Hearst newspapers. Hearst went further than that. After a quick look through the book, he sent his two-word order to Connolly.

Connolly's own editorial and publishing genius was one big reason why Ripley went with King Features rather than with one of the other syndicates pursuing him. It was Connolly who came across a novel printed in Germany and, over the objections of his colleagues, arranged for its serialization in the United States. And the book, *All Quiet on the Western Front*, later hailed as a major novel, became one of the most successful serializations of all time. It was Connolly who spotted the one-day appearance of an illiterate but honest sailor in Elzie Segar's fading comic strip, "Thimble Theater." "Feature the sailor," Connolly told Segar, and "Popeye" went on to comic-strip glory. It was Connolly who inspired Chic Young to develop "Blondie," and then, in order to expand syndication, sent silk panties with copies of the strip to thousands of newspaper editors around the world. Ripley knew about Connolly—and what he and the Hearst organization could do for an artist.

This was the turning point in Robert L. Ripley's life. With the limited syndication he enjoyed before signing with KFS, Ripley earned about $10,000 in 1928. He could and did live well by most standards, but in niggardly fashion compared with what was to come. In 1930 his earnings were upward of $100,000, and at the very bottom of the depression, a few years later, his income reached $500,000 annually—an exalted level at which it was maintained by revenues from radio shows, lectures, freak shows, movies, and countless other ventures. Suddenly Ripley could indulge his every whim, and there were some dandies.

Connolly always insisted that Ripley himself was his own greatest oddity. Ripley acquired a baronial twenty-nine-room home on his own island, and kept a twenty-eight-foot boa constrictor there as a pet. He had a huge apartment in Manhattan and a palatial home in Palm Beach. He stocked and maintained a full-blown harem, and at various times there were as many as a dozen women residing in one or another of his castles—ethnic products of China, Japan, the Soviet Union, France, Greece, and Germany. He cruised the world— earning the title of "Modern Marco Polo"—with a retinue as exotic as that of any Oriental potentate.

For journeys in United States territorial waters Rip purchased an authentic Chinese junk so overly powered with twin diesels that at full speed—which was the only speed Rip recognized—the patched old sail of the magnificent vessel billowed *backward;* and many a tipsy Long Island Sound seafarer was jolted into sobriety as Ripley's junk roared by, sail working at cross-purposes, deck covered with the Caliph's sun-bathing babes.

He lived it up, this strange, mixed-up man. He would own the most expensive foreign cars obtainable, but never summon up enough courage to drive. He would pioneer in transatlantic radio broadcasting, but he would never dial a telephone, because in his curious mind there lurked the suspicion that he might be electrocuted in the process. He consumed enormous quantities of liquor and may have set a record for amorous dalliance, but he considered smoking and card playing evil and would have nothing to do with them. He was, to those who knew him best, the very personification of shyness, but no contemporary matched him in flamboyance or in seeking notoriety.

Ripley and "Believe It or Not" became household words in fourteen languages and thirty countries where the cartoon was syndicated—and a readership survey in the United States once showed that it topped every feature in reader interest with the single exception of first page news. "That's one for Ripley," and, "Tell It to Ripley" passed into the language just as "Annie Oakley" and "the real McCoy." His newspaper audience was estimated in excess of seventy-five million readers. And it seemed as though at one time or another all of them wrote to him; his mail reached the staggering average of a million letters a year, and, in one *week*, while he was conducting a contest to find "Believe It or Nots," hit 465,000. His fame was such that letters merely ripped, to indicate that they should go to "Rip," would reach him. And his appeal as a collector of the odd, weird, grotesque, amazing, and peculiar was so powerful that his radio and TV shows were successful for nearly two decades, despite a mumbling, fumbling, stumbling start, compounded of simple mike fright and gross ineptitude.

The golden public triumphs were interwoven in Rip's life with personal failures of an increasingly somber hue. The gap between public success and private tragedy, in fact, seemed to widen steadily from 1929, when he was propelled toward his greatest heights as a cartoonist, collector, performer, and entrepreneur. He would travel a long, long way from a boyhood of poverty in Santa Rosa, California. He would travel a million miles or more and return to Santa Rosa in death, without finding whatever it was he had been seeking, or realizing fully where he had been.

CHAPTER II

Horatio and the Harem

THE early years of LeRoy Ripley, who was destined to live like a twentieth-century sultan, were strictly Horatio Alger. All the required ingredients were present: the small-town locale, a boy with great ambition and enormous drive, the widowed mother, the kind benefactor, and the big break. Ripley later tried to embellish the facts—for example, he changed his birth date from December 26, 1893, to December 25—but the facts themselves should have been more than enough.

Santa Rosa was a town of about 5000 population in Ripley's time. It was the market place for a lush valley producing wine and wool. Sheep grazed on the beautiful green hills that protected the valley from the cold wet winds of the Pacific. Santa Rosa had a woolen mill, a gasworks, banks, two newspapers, a new city hall, and Luther Burbank, the "Wizard" of plant breeding.

LeRoy's mother was born Lilly Belle Yucca in a covered wagon on the old Santa Fe trail. Her husband, Isaac Davis Ripley, born of old American stock in West Virginia, had run away from home at the age of fourteen to seek fame and fortune in California. Along the way he swam the Ohio River, because he didn't have the price of a ferryboat ride. He died in 1905—having found neither fame nor fortune and leaving the house he had built with his own hands and three young children: LeRoy, twelve, Ethel, and Douglas, a toddler.

Mrs. Ripley, a small, wiry, and strong-willed woman, partly of Portuguese descent, met the problem of rearing and educating the family by taking up practical nursing, renting rooms in her home, and turning to needlework and other occasional chores. LeRoy, a tall, skinny boy with buck teeth, pitched in to augment the family income. His first job, working after school hours and on Saturday, was polishing headstones for the Fisher & Kinslow marble works—he left because it was "too gloomy." He also helped load fruit and vegetable wagons and did an occasional paint job on a neighbor's porch.

Ripley had plenty of energy left over, and found two primary outlets for it: the drawing board and the athletic field. Completely self-taught, he had been drawing as early as anyone in the house could remember, starting with crayons. At Santa Rosa High, the shy and quiet boy did cartoons for the school paper, the *Porcupine*, and even went so far as to turn in some of his assigned homework themes in the form of illustrated stories. He had trouble then and for many years later expressing himself as forcefully as he wished in the more conventional ways.

Whenever he could find a ball game, whether at school or in the neighborhood, Ripley managed to get into it. As is the case with most teen-agers of exceptional baseball ability, he was a pitcher. In the professional ranks, few pitchers even qualify as athletes, being more or less physical freaks with specialized skills, but among kids the best all-around athlete in the group usually is the pitcher. That was Ripley, a splendid athlete through much of his life.

Needing money to help support his family, Ripley managed to combine his two chief interests and make them pay. He pitched semipro ball when he was thirteen and drew posters advertising the games for use in shop windows. He earned as much as $15.00 a week this way, a great deal of money for a teen-ager.

In 1907, at the age of fourteen, the die was cast for his future. He sold a cartoon to the old *Life* magazine and got a check for $8.00. It was the first cartoon he had ever submitted to a major periodical, and his instant success convinced him that he would be an artist. This drawing showed some young women washing clothes and was entitled "The Village Belles Were Slowly Wringing."

In the summer of 1908 Carol Ennis came to Santa Rosa to visit her mother, who had taken a room at the Ripley home for a vacation. Carol had been doing Sunday-supplement features for the old San Francisco *Call* and had married Earle Ennis in 1900. Ennis for thirty-five years was a columnist for the *Bulletin* and *Chronicle*, and, later, for the Oakland *Tribune;* and Carol then, and for years after, enjoyed a close association with the fourth estate.

With her San Francisco background of newspapers, Carol also had a side attachment for art. She had been a student in an organization which, if its title is any criterion, must have been highly informal, even for artists. It was known as the One-Dinner-a-Week-Montgomery-Street Art Group.

The association of Mrs. Ennis with artists, nebulous as it was, attracted the skinny Ripley boy. He was emboldened to show Carol, some ten years his senior, sketches he had made for the school newspaper and semipro posters. In his bold strokes and violent, vibrant action, Mrs. Ennis detected what she was sure was budding genius. Ripley's energy was being worked off in his drawings.

Carol thought the fifteen-year-old Ripley's talent deserved a wider field than the pages of the school paper and posters in cigar-store windows. He should be on one of the San

Francisco papers. This was a presidential year, with William Howard Taft and William Jennings Bryan opposing each other. Carol decided that a political cartoon would be the quickest way to open the door for this embryo Rembrandt, and approached him on the subject.

"Do you know anything about politics, Roy?" she asked.

"Not a thing," answered Ripley cheerfully.

In what must have been one of the most intensive political seminars of all time, Mrs. Ennis sat down with Roy to work out a theme for a cartoon on the presidential race. Ripley executed it, and Carol set out for San Francisco with this and several of Roy's sports cartoons.

The enthusiasm Mrs. Ennis held for young Ripley's ability was not shared noticeably by any of the San Francisco editors to whom she showed his work. Far from being discouraged, Carol decided on a flanking attack. With the aid of her husband, she began working on newspaper friends of theirs to intercede on Ripley's behalf.

In the beginning this plan made no marked headway. Managing editors have been impervious to suggestions since the days of the runic alphabet. Discovering that broadsides were getting them nowhere, the Ennises decided to concentrate their fire on a single target.

Frank Muligrew, a friend of the Ennises, was the man who stepped into the breach. He agreed to an all-out, nonstop assault on Jim Bagerley of the *Bulletin*. It finally worked, and Roy got his chance at something like $18 a week.

Although the Taft-Bryan cartoon had been drawn expressly for the purpose of opening the journalistic doors for Ripley, Bagerley decided that politics was not the young man's forte, an opinion wholeheartedly shared by Ripley's friends for the rest of his life. The sports cartoons, however, did impress Bagerley, as did Rip's unchallenged knowledge of baseball.

It was decided that the youngster should do a series on semi-pro baseball.

San Francisco, even five decades before Candlestick Park, was a hotbed of baseball enthusiasm. The Bay Area frequently supported as many as three clubs in the Pacific Coast League—two in San Francisco and one in Oakland—but even this heavy representation in the highest minor league in the country didn't wholly satisfy the appetite of the natives for baseball. Semipro clubs functioned in all sections of the city, and Ripley's cartoons served to boost the *Bulletin*'s circulation.

The Ripley who embarked on a newspaper career was still in his teens, a tall, skinny kid, good-looking except for his buck teeth, and shy.

One of the few stories Ripley told about his early days in the newspaper business goes a long way toward explaining why his shyness clung to him until so late in life. Gawky, uncultured, self-conscious about his buck teeth, Rip tried to protect himself against social *faux pas* by avoiding social life.

"I had an experience when I first went to San Francisco which I'll never forget," he once told me. "It was the custom there for the cartoonists on the various papers to do an occasional cover for *The Chaparral*, the student magazine of Stanford University.

"One day I brought a cover over to the editor and he asked me to wait in his dormitory room while he attended to some other business. I noticed a pair of silver-backed military brushes on his dresser. I had never seen anything like them before and I picked them up and began shining my shoes with them. The student editor returned and was properly horrified. All I could do was blush and stammer my way out of the room. I couldn't tell him that I thought they were shoe-brushes."

To overcome his shyness, Ripley had a major asset going for him: talent. He was a first-rate sports cartoonist before he was out of his teens. He had to be, to compete in San Francisco, for that city in the early years of this century spawned the nation's finest practitioners of the art. There was Thomas A. Dorgan, known to millions as "TAD"; Rube Goldberg, who later relinquished sports in favor of "Boob McNutt" and his weird comic inventions; Paul Terry, creator of the animated movie series, "Terrytoons"; Hype Igoe, who achieved greater glory as a sports writer, and "Bud" Fisher, later kingpin of all comic artists with his "Mutt and Jeff" strip.

The four years that Ripley spent in San Francisco were crammed with excitement, not the least of which came from mingling with the "greats" of his trade. He covered the Jack Johnson-Jim Jeffries heavyweight title fight at Reno on July 4, 1910, a prize assignment for a youngster. At ringside he met two distinguished men of letters, Jack London and Peter B. Kyne, who thought enough of Ripley to help him move from the *Bulletin* to the *Chronicle* for a couple of dollars a week more. And each of these men in his own way opened new worlds for Ripley.

Ripley was properly awed by Jack London, the outstanding figure of a San Francisco literary explosion that produced Gertrude Atherton, the prolific Norris family, Kyne, and others. London was only thirty-four years old when Ripley met him, but Ripley and others of his generation gazed upon London as they would some distant star. London's income in the year 1910 was reputed to be $75,000. He was completing "Wolf's Head," the fabulous ranch and house at Glen Ellen, in Sonoma County. London—to Ripley, particularly—was the poor boy who had achieved everything there was to achieve —he had fame, fortune, adventure, lavish living. That he was a miserably unhappy man, unable to curb his drinking and extravagant spending, moving from one love affair to another, Ripley did not know. He was deeply impressed by London's style of living, including, among other things, an Oriental servant, and he quite clearly set out to imitate it years later when he himself had the fame and fortune.

Ripley's native taste for adventure and the exotic were fed not only by people like Jack London but by San Francisco as it was during his time. When he was not working, he spent a great deal of his time walking the streets from one side of town to another, stirred by the beauty, vigor, and excitement of the place. Increasingly he devoted his leisure to China-town—partly because he could eat cheaply there (and there wasn't much of his salary left after he sent money to his mother), but also because of the way it nurtured his imagination.

Sitting around in the dim little Chinese restaurants, Ripley heard, firsthand, stories of an alien, exotic land. China at that time was still relatively untouched by Western civilization and it could still be called by its quaint, lovely name of Cathay. The old storytellers, dressed in their long gowns, still wearing queues, smoking their slender reed pipes, awoke in Ripley a vision and affection that the passing years would only intensify. He constantly insisted that the Chinese were "the only truly civilized people."

Accepting the Chinese civilization as a highly desirable state of affairs, Ripley acquired some attitudes toward women that proved, in later years, to be, at the very least, anachronistic. Young Ripley saw the rich, arrogant concubine with her face powdered into a mask and her gleaming black hair piled on her head like an intricate bit of masonry. He saw the tired little singsong girls, who never knew youth, used and despised by the fat, shrewd merchants. The Chinese of that time generally did not bring their wives to the United States,

1

Ripley's big house, Bion, on New York's Long Island Sound. Rip loved the house, and used it for this Christmas card.

Ripley's cartoons had wider circulation than any author has ever had with the printed word—three thousand newspapers in fourteen languages.

UNITED PRESS INTERNATIONAL PHOTO

Hazel Storer and Florence Keesely "clown" with the exotic carvings and totems at Bion.

A cocktail party at Ripley's winter estate, "Hi-Mount," Palm Beach, Florida.

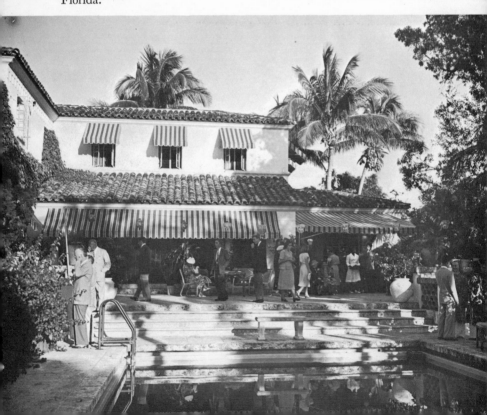

Ripley is host at a typical Chinese dinner given at his fantastic New York apartment.

Back home from the Orient in 1948, Ripley spreads out on the floor of his New York apartment the Chinese stamps needed to send an air-mail letter from inflation-torn Shanghai to New York.

Ripley gives Hazel and Doug Storer a wedding reception at his New York apartment. Ripley's good "right hand," Bill McDonald, pours an exotic marriage wine.

Ripley's colorful Chinese junk, the *Mon-Lei*, under full sail in Long Island Sound.

but occasionally Ripley would see one, hobbling about on cruelly deformed "lily-pad" feet, bound from birth in an ancient exercise of vanity.

While eating in a Chinese restaurant in San Francisco one night, Ripley was introduced by some newspaper friends to a man who was to have a profound effect upon his future, one Joe Taylor, a rather undistinguished actor who had written an autobiography entitled *Joe Taylor, Barnstormer* and was looking for someone to illustrate it. Taylor had long since retired and was living in Woodlands, California. Rip was surprised and delighted to learn that Taylor had appeared as an actor in China shortly after the American Civil War.

Ripley had a dual interest in Taylor. He was fascinated by the veteran actor's stories of the adventure of a white man in China in the nineteenth century and he was impressed with the possibility of picking up some extra money by illustrating his autobiography. It was no princely sum—$100 for twenty illustrations—but it was enough eventually to send Ripley to New York.

One of the twenty pictures Ripley produced for Taylor's book was the first of many cartoons he was to do with a Chinese motif. This was captioned "An Early Morning Shave in Bed" and showed a pigtailed barber shaving a man (Taylor) with a meat cleaver.

The decision of Ripley to challenge New York was not a sudden one. Years before the Golden Gate lured Horace Stoneham and the New York Giants westward from the lee of Coogan's Bluff, there was a steady procession of talent reversing the advice of Horace Greeley and streaming eastward from the Bay Area, including "TAD," Terry, Goldberg, and Herb Roth.

Seeing his contemporaries go off to New York and hearing tales of their success made Ripley impatient. He asked for a

$5.00 raise and was promptly fired by the *Chronicle*. He went to Kyne for help. Kyne was then about thirty years old and had an established reputation which would gain a greater luster as he poured out his "Cappy Ricks" stories. Ripley told him, "I'm a failure just when I'm getting started. What should I do?" Kyne suggested that he head for New York. And the $100 Ripley obtained from Taylor for illustrating his book was enough to get him there.

The list of Ripley benefactors, starting with Carol Ennis and including Muligrew, London, and Kyne—people who were attracted to him by both his shy gawkiness and his talent—quickly lengthened when he hit New York in 1913. In a biography of J. N. (Ding) Darling by Tom Mahoney in the *Saturday Evening Post* in 1940, Ripley's arrival in the big town is thus re-created:

"To the office [George Matthew Adams' syndicate in the old *Globe*] also came one day an awkward nineteen-year-old boy fresh from San Francisco in an army shirt and trousers cuffed halfway to the knee. Distrusting subways, he had trudged many blocks with a bundle of sports cartoons. These impressed no artist in the office except Ding, who was enthusiastic over a certain boldness of stroke in a sketch of a baseball player. 'The boy's got something,' Darling told the snydicate manager. 'Hire him for six months and I will pay his salary.' Darling didn't have to pay. The boy was Robert L. (*Believe It or Not*) Ripley, destined to become one of the highest paid newspaper artists of all time."

He was named LeRoy Ripley, and the Robert was added to the beginning later, with LeRoy reduced to a middle initial. Sometimes Rip said the addition to his name had been accomplished in San Francisco, but the evidence is to the contrary. All his friends from the Coast continued to call him Roy, as did those who knew him in his first years in New York.

Ripley came to a leisurely New York in 1913. Everything was cheap. Nobody had heard the word "inflation" since the post-Civil War period, and that graphic term "rat race" had not yet been coined.

Ripley, now that he had a steady income, soon took up residence in a flat—they hadn't started calling them apartments yet—on West Sixty-fifth Street in what in those days was known as "the first floor back," which meant that the tenant had an unobstructed view of the back yard for his $35 a month rent. Today it would be called a garden apartment and would be considerably more expensive. The $35 rent was the key to Bob's living. An instant success as a sports cartoonist after he joined the *Globe*, Ripley soon was making about $100 a week. He was able to send money regularly to his mother until her death in 1915. He had no financial worries, no struggle for existence, and no overwork. Life was real but far from earnest.

Ripley naturally gravitated to a set which included many of his acquaintances from San Francisco, as well as natives and outlanders whose company he found enjoyable. The group, which might best be described as successful Bohemians, a far cry from the beatniks of today, had as its focal point the Sunday-night salons of Helena Dayton Smith, who designed tiny figurines of exquisite beauty.

Here gathered Paul Terry and Herb Roth, who had preceded Ripley in the hegira from the Coast, as well as humorist Arthur (Bugs) Baer, who became Rip's closest friend. Others were Marcus Cook Connelly, who was to become a top Broadway name as a playwright and collaborator; Montague Glass, humorist and playwright; Ray Rohan, Berton Braley, and Vyvyan Donner, a free-lance artist.

An evening on the town in those years immediately preceding the entrance of the United States into World War I placed no particular strain on the exchequer. Ripley, Terry, and some of his other cronies were habitués of Poggi's, an Italian restaurant on West Twenty-ninth Street, almost at the Hudson River, which had among its patrons the great Enrico Caruso. You could get a full-course dinner and a bottle of red wine for something under a dollar, and everybody seemed satisfied.

Between the dollar dinner and the Sunday-night sessions at Miss Smith's, Ripley felt he was living a full life. Essentially shy, Bob enjoyed listening but could talk when drawn into the conversation, and displayed the same lively mind which was to distinguish his "Believe It or Not" feature.

"We had some wonderful gatherings at Helena's," recalled Miss Donner, now fashion editor for Fox Movietonews. "Bugs Baer was then, as he is today, one of the most humorous and sharpest persons I have ever met. Paul Terry had a quick wit, and Herb Roth was the perfect foil, always underplaying the remark in a dry, droll way.

"There was nothing which could be called heavy drinking in those days," she continued. "That came with the advent of Prohibition. When I had dinner with Roy, or any of my other beaux, as we called them then, a couple of drinks took care of the entire evening. You and your escort would have a cocktail before dinner, dance a while and order another drink an hour or so later, and that would be it."

Ripley, on the basis of his practically instant success as a sports cartoonist, changed quickly and drastically from the gangling boy in the army shirt and foreshortened trousers that Ding Darling first glimpsed in the *Globe* office. The attire he adopted was considered peculiar, to say the least, even among the carefree set with which he traveled. His startling color combinations caused Bugs Baer to exclaim when he first encountered Ripley in one of his wilder getups, "He looks like a paint factory that got hit by lightning!"

From the bottom up, Ripley's ensemble on any given one of those prewar days would include two-toned shoes, the tips polished to a dazzling shine; a black-and-white hound's-tooth check suit; pale pink pleated shirt; and the inevitable multi-colored batwing tie. The Ripley of later years would make no discernible headway toward becoming a well-dressed man in the conventional sense. In fact, he always preferred the pith helmet and suntan shorts, or coolie shirts, or Eskimo parkas that his world-ranging travels seemed to dictate.

Little more than a year after Ripley arrived in New York, he took the first of his countless trips abroad, disturbing evidence that there was in him an uncontrollable restlessness. For here he was, just barely established in the world's greatest metropolis, only twenty-one years old, dressing well (by his own lights) for the first time, moving in an exciting and entertaining circle of friends, and he was off to Europe. As it turned out, this first year in New York was just about the longest stay-put period of his adult life, in which he visited some two hundred countries.

That first trip in 1914 was a modest one by later Ripley standards. He traveled, "with one suitcase and a round-trip ticket," as he described it, to London, Paris, and Rome and was gone about four and a half weeks. During this period Ripley still thought about being a "serious" artist and went to Europe primarily to visit the great museums. What he saw there either left him cold or convinced him that he did not have the kind of talent required. He was never thereafter very interested in the fine arts; snorted at "modern" paintings, and collected only the huge and spectacular.

Returning from Europe, Bob left his West Sixty-fifth Street flat and moved into an apartment with Paul Terry on West

Fiftieth Street between Fifth and Sixth avenues. This apartment, in a brownstone front, consisted of a large front room,
which Ripley used as a studio, and a smaller rear room, with
two cots, which served as the bedroom. Since Terry did all his
work in his office, Ripley had the studio to himself.

The pattern of Ripley's life was set in these early years in
New York, although he added some extravagant touches; it
was essentially: work hard, play hard, and keep on the move.
In his first job on the *Globe* and with the George Matthew
Adams syndicate, he had the benefit of working alongside
some exceptionally talented men. Among them, besides Ding
Darling, were H. T. Webster, who created "The Timid Soul,"
and Percy Crosby, who brought "Skippy" to life. Ripley
studied them closely, but he worked very hard at developing
his own bold, dashing cartoon style, and he took great pride
in it.

Away from his drawing board, Ripley turned most often to
Bugs Baer as a companion in the fun available to young men
in New York at the time. Like Ripley, Baer started his career
as a sports cartoonist, first working in Philadelphia and Washington and arriving in New York at about the same time as
his great good friend-to-be. (He acquired his nickname by
implanting in his cartoons, as his trade-mark, a couple of tiny
bugs.) While Ripley was on the *Globe,* Bugs drew for the New
York *World,* which boasted as its top sports page attraction
the nonpareil of sports cartooning, Bob Edgren. Bugs never
thought of himself as in Edgren's class as a cartoonist, but
almost everyone who ever read or heard Bugs knew he was
a very funny man. What the world lost when Bugs gave up
cartooning it gained in his occasional stints as vaudevillian
and in his columns—including some of the most memorable
lines of humor ever to enliven a stage or newspaper page. It
was Bugs who first uttered what was for many years the per-

fect squelch: "How much would you charge to haunt a house?" It was Bugs who wrote of a notoriously slow-footed baseball player who attempted, in a fit of frenzy, to steal second base and was thrown out by a country mile: "Ping Bodie's head was full of larceny, but his feet were honest." And it was Bugs who described a slow-witted fellow this way: "He was so dumb they had to tear down the schoolhouse to get him out of second grade."

Ripley and Baer, although close friends, were also rivals in a wide variety of competitive sports: handball, drinking, walking, attracting girls, and wrestling (each other). Word of the latter reached a shrewd sports promoter named Jack Curley just at a time, in December 1916, when he was badly in need of an attraction to beef up a wrestling card scheduled for the old Lexington Avenue opera house. Curley was a man of great charm and even greater guile. He went to Ripley and told him, "Bugs says he can throw you; will you wrestle him for me?" From Ripley came an expletive or two and a "Th'ell he can!" which Curley loosely translated as throwing down the gantlet to Baer. He carried that challenge to Baer and the match was forthwith arranged.

Ripley and Baer were first billed as the semi-windup to a contest between Stanislaus Zbyszko and Ed (Strangler) Lewis. But sports-writing friends so effectively built up their combat as a "grudge match" likely to produce gross mayhem that Rip and Bugs became the headliners, although neither could have survived ten seconds with Lewis or Zbyszko. For one thing, Bugs, the heavier of the pair by a couple of pounds, weighed in at a ring-splintering 148. For another, neither had too much to offer except a certain agility and enthusiasm. Curley couldn't do anything about the former deficiency except lie, but he attempted to give his headliners at least a bit of professional polish, dispatching them to a jujitsu expert named Ralph Bingham. After a half-hour session with Bingham, each had half mastered a half nelson and a headlock and was ready for the big event.

Wrestling in those days was still on the up and up, with feigned kicks, bites, butts, and similar refinements yet to come. It was a mixture of Greco-Roman and catch as catch can, and it was dull as dust even to devotees unless practiced at a high level of competence. Curley—ahead of his time—decided that the match had to be fixed, and since Ripley and Baer fell, roughly, into the hero and villain categories, Rip was to be the winner in two straight falls lasting about eleven minutes each. The purse was $75 each.

The Lexington opera house was packed. George Bothner, who had been world middleweight wrestling champ, was the referee. Sid Mercer, perhaps the best all-around sports writer of them all, was the timekeeper. The front of the stage was roped off to make a ring. Things were going more or less according to plan for the first seven or eight minutes, with the combatants applying alternate half nelsons and headlocks, at which point Ripley had pushed Baer's head into the footlights. Bugs' discomfort was intensified beyond endurance when he heard a feminine voice demanding, "Throw the bum! Throw him!" Bugs managed to lift his head enough to see where the voice was coming from—a beautiful young woman with a beautiful young woman alongside.

"Who d'ya mean?" Bugs demanded.

"You, y'bum," he was told. At which point Baer forgot the plan by which Ripley would win.

Actually, neither man was capable of winning, a melancholy thought that swept over the audience as Rip and Bugs hugged and tugged and pushed and wheezed. The crowd became increasingly restive. Referee Bothner leaned over to the men and hissed, "Do something different! For God's sake, do something different!"

Bugs looked up at him and said, "Bring out the hook."

That was enough for Bothner, and for a dozen members of the audience, who rose to their feet and headed uncertainly for the ring. Bothner dashed into the wings, and was replaced for the remaining few seconds of the match by timekeeper Mercer. Mercer was succeeded suddenly by two policemen, summoned on threat of a riot. The cops hustled Ripley and Baer offstage, but not until Rip had called to the pair of front-row beauties to meet him at the side door.

In their natural desire to spruce up for the girls after the grimy match, Rip and Bugs made a serious mistake. They went searching around the opera house for a shower, thereby permitting promoter Curley to make his exit—with the night's receipts. When Rip sought out Curley a few days later he was told, "I gave the whole hundred and fifty to Baer. He said he'd handle your end for you." At the same time, he sent word to Bugs that Ripley had collected for both of them. It is a measure of Curley's skill that, although Bugs and Ripley remained very close friends for the next thirty-three years, neither was absolutely convinced the other wasn't richer by an extra $75; and a dozen years after Ripley's death Bugs ruminatively told the writer, "Only thing I'm really certain of is that *I* never got a nickel."

Sports were always a big part of Ripley's life. Covering spring training of the New York Giants at Marlin, Texas, Rip worked out with the club daily and made an impression on John McGraw. At one point Mac spoke seriously with Rip about a career in professional baseball, telling him that with a few years in the minors he might very well become a big-league prospect. Eddie Brannick, something of a "Believe It or Not" himself, in that he joined the Giants in 1904 as an office manager and was still with them fifty-seven years later, saw Ripley at those Marlin training camps and described him as a pitcher of considerable promise and ability.

Ripley also knew a good deal about athletes and athletics —necessarily, because he was called upon to draw a sports cartoon for the *Globe* five days a week. These were of a conventional nature and angled to the news: two or three glimpses of a current baseball hero from different angles or in different poses; the story of a boxing title contender's life told in three or four sketches. But Ripley also was attracted to the unusual and curious in sports. Apparently with nothing particular in mind, he had been collecting bizarre sports items for a couple of years. At least he never mentioned them to anyone until December 18, 1918 when he found himself barren of ideas for his sports cartoon as the afternoon wore on and the hour approached for a scheduled date with a current favorite, Beatrice Roberts, a onetime Massachusetts beauty-contest winner who was dancing in a Ned Wayburn show.

In place of the usual cartoon for the next day's paper Ripley assembled nine unusual sports events in small sketches. They included the following intelligence: "J. Darby of England Jumped Backwards 12 ft. 11 in. (with weights)"; "R. P. Williams Made a Running High Kick of 10 ft. 3 in. (New London, Conn.—1905)"; "H. Hillman and Lawson Robertson did 100 yds. in 11 secs. in a three-legged race"; "Remember The Chap Who Walked Backwards Across The Continent?" (those who didn't got no help from Ripley other than a sketch of a man with a stick in one hand and a mirror in the other in a walking pose); "M. Pauliquen, Paris—1912 remained under water 6 min. 29 ⅖ secs."; "Ed Lamy broad-jumped on ice 25 ft. 7 in. (Saranac Lake 1913)"; "S. D. See Hopped 100 yds. in 11 seconds"; "A. Forrester of Toronto—ran 100 yds. Backwards in

14 seconds"; "J. M. Barnett of Australia Jumped the Rope 11,180 times (about 4 hours)."

Ripley captioned this hodgepodge "Champs and Chumps" and placed it on the desk of Walter St. Denis, the *Globe*'s sports editor. St. Denis, a round little man with watery blue eyes and tousled iron-gray hair, approved of the cartoon in general but was cold toward the caption, pointing out to the cartoonist that the characters he had depicted and the feats they had performed made them neither champs nor chumps, but "just guys who did some screwy athletic stunts."

There was further consultation over a more suitable caption, and finally "Believe It or Not" was born. Whether St. Denis or Ripley sired the new title is a matter of debate, but it was a most happy choice. It was to become far more of a trademark for Ripley than his buck teeth or his batwing ties. The phrase was to become part of the American language, more enduring than Ripley himself.

Here again was evidence of the manner in which the gods worked with Ripley. "Champs and Chumps" as a title would never have captured the public's fancy as did "Believe It or Not." Few are the recorded instances in history where fame and fortune came to a man because he couldn't do his proper day's work—in this instance, thinking up an idea for a sports cartoon. Ripley's place in the American scene was founded on a substitute caption for a makeshift cartoon.

It is significant that Ripley himself didn't give the cartoon a second thought. When the new caption was acceptable, Bob was out of the office and on his way to his date. He was as surprised as anybody else when letters began to trickle into the *Globe* suggesting that the *Globe*'s readers would like more of the same.

The letters impressed St. Denis. He called Ripley to his desk a day or so later. "Maybe you could do another of those screwy cartoons, Rip," said Walter, "if you can think up some more crazy stunts to use in it."

Ripley had little difficulty in getting together enough "crazy stunts" to satisfy St. Denis, and the second of the "screwy" cartoons caught on even more widely than the first. St. Denis decided to make it a weekly feature. Soon "Believe It or Not" appeared twice a week, and then as a daily feature.

The first "Believe It or Not" probably has been reproduced more often than Da Vinci's *Mona Lisa*. It has appeared in all of Ripley's books, which, in their many editions, have sold in the millions. It is somewhat significant that in his later books the caption "Champs and Chumps" disappeared. Early reproductions of the original showed the first title crossed out and "Believe It or Not" blocked in above it. Maybe Bob didn't care to be reminded of the narrow margin by which he could have missed the boat.

The inertia and instability which marked Ripley's approach to his first brush with the printed word were to remain with him throughout his life. When he was an established star in the Hearst galaxy, he gave serious thought to deserting that employer for another, Christy Walsh, an independent promoter and personal management genius.

Walsh is generally credited in sports with being the inventor of the press-box ghost, the by-lined story of an athlete about a contest in which he is participating. There may have been ghost stories on the sports pages before the emergence of Walsh—indeed, all the evidence is that there were—but incontrovertibly it was Christy who put the spectral typewriters on a paying basis.

Walsh was the personal manager of Babe Ruth and Lou Gehrig, as well as dozens of lesser-known athletes, from prize fighters to Ivy League football coaches. About the time Ruth was beginning to fade as a player, Christy, who was well known to Ripley, approached Bob with the idea of taking him under his promotional wing.

There was no questioning the ability of Walsh. He had a flair for promotion and had demonstrated it in the large sums he brought, not only to the athletes whose by-lines he acquired, but to the ink-stained wretches who ground out the copy of the sweaty authors. Christy, however, was a one-man show, while Hearst represented a nationwide organization. Nevertheless, Ripley was intrigued with the thought of moving out from Hearst.

Ripley sought out his close friend, Baer, for advice. Under the Hearst banner, Bugs had blossomed into the nation's number-one wit. Baer listened carefully while Ripley told of what he thought Walsh could do for him. Finally Bugs rendered his decision.

Choosing between Walsh and Hearst, Bugs said, was like choosing between Jimmy Johnston, a sports promoter who operated out of his brown Derby hat, and the far more solid and successful Tex Rickard, operator of Madison Square Garden.

"Stick to Hearst, Bob," Baer advised. "He's got a building. If anything goes wrong you can sue him and attach all his doorknobs."

CHAPTER III

Determined Bachelor

TRYING to understand Bob Ripley's curious relationship with women—with a veritable host of women of all types, ages, complexions, and attitudes—is among the more perplexing jobs facing any biographer. Over the years he played the roles of dutiful son, ardent lover, slave master, platonic friend, big brother, and harem operator. But he always seemed fiercely determined to avoid any permanent, constant alliance with any one woman, marital or otherwise. He became unusually adept at the bachelor talent of broken field running, and he was trapped into marriage—or trapped himself—only once.

Rip, in fact, could have written the manual on bachelorhood for the period just after World War I. He had money, he was a "snappy" dresser, he learned to dance well, he was physically attractive—despite his buck teeth—and he lived the part. Rip maintained bachelor quarters in the New York Athletic Club starting in 1918, made a point of meeting Bugs Baer, Herb Roth, Paul Terry, or other of his friends for a drink or meal at Perry's Gluepot or The Times Café, and kept his evenings free for the eternal chase. The locale of the latter might be Churchill's Café on Broadway, Rector's, Healey's Golden Glades for ice skating, or, fairly often, the stage door of one of Broadway's seventy-five theaters.

Thus it was that Rip's friends were startled to discover early in 1919 that he was married to Beatrice Roberts. If he hadn't told them, nonchalantly, some of them might never have known. For the marriage did little to change the pattern and tempo of his life, and it lasted only a few months.

Rip had been dating Beatrice Roberts for about a year. She was tall, blond, and Junoesque, about nineteen years old, a lovely showgirl and model. But he had been dating other lovely young things too. In announcing to his friends the change in status, he simply said, "We're married," and never looked particularly happy about it. Actually his wife had considerably more reason for unhappiness.

Ripley did condescend in the interests of matrimonial harmony to give up his place at the New York Athletic Club briefly and take a suite with his bride at the Tavern, an inn on West Forty-eighth Street in Manhattan. But that was about all of his liberty that he surrendered. A bug on physical condition, Rip had been making regular visits to a fight camp in New Jersey operated by an Englishman named Thomas; he did road work with the fighters, and followed the same strict training regimen they did, stopping short only of entering the ring. This routine he continued after the marriage.

The new Mrs. Ripley, curiously enough, didn't take to the idea of her hubby moving out to a fight camp, despite assurances that it was operated along strictly monastic lines. She was constantly on the telephone to him, wondering about his dealings with the wife of a trainer who was living in a cottage just a short distance away from the fight camp itself. Mrs. Ripley had never seen the woman or she would have had no worries, for the gal who might have been the third point of the triangle was a hatchet-faced crone twice Ripley's age. And Ripley himself insisted that he had never seen her. But, as a general statement, it would be hard to fault Mrs. Ripley for being suspicious of almost any female with whom he might come in contact.

There were times in the stormy marriage when it appeared that Ripley was in training in New Jersey for the fights at home. His wife was a woman of strong temper and not to be pushed around. They had violent arguments. And after about three months the marriage was over, although Mrs. Ripley didn't get a divorce until 1925.

As was so often true of Ripley's shattered romances, he and Beatrice got along much more amicably after they were separated. They were friends before and after she remarried. And this is part of the record that shows Ripley to be much more successful in his platonic, or nonromantic, associations with women.

Rip always showed deep respect for Carol Ennis, who had landed him his first newspaper job. No matter where he traveled, he sent her gifts and a note, always signed, "Ever devotedly, Rip." And he inscribed one of his books to her this way:

> *But for the grace of Carol,*
> *There goes Rip to Santa Rosa!*

He was a friend of Vyvyan Donner for some thirty-five years. Toward her he demonstrated warmth and serious concern for her well-being, taking an interest in her career, in her travels, in where and how she lived. On every important occasion in his life—a new book, a new radio show, a big trip—he went to talk to her, to get her opinions.

But these were comparatively uncomplicated relationships for Ripley. Each of the women had inner resources that made her independent of him. Neither was out to entrap him, to fence him in. There were no everyday demands on him. So Rip could feel completely comfortable with them.

And because the relationships were comparatively uncomplicated, Rip did not distort them in portraying them to others. In most of the more bizarre affairs in his life Rip tended to add an element or dimension of drama or melodrama. It became extremely difficult to tell which women, if any, he may actually have been in love with—there were certainly not more than a few, out of the dozens or hundreds in his life. Even for close friends, it was difficult to determine the truth of certain romantic interludes he related, although the truth would always have been interesting enough.

The most astonishing "Believe It or Not" of all that Ripley ever produced was one he reserved for a small circle of friends —and it is fair to say that not all of them accepted the story without some inner doubts. It involved a statuesque girl named Doris, with whom Rip had a brief but serious romance shortly after World War I. Some thought that he might marry her.

In the early 1930s Ripley became interested in the Mayan Indians and decided to travel to Yucatán, for the usual combination of reasons: to keep on the move, to seek out new items for his feature, and to dwell among the exotic. Bugs Baer arranged through friends of his connected with a coastwise steamship line to get Ripley aboard a small banana boat which carried a handful of passengers. The master was a Captain Blackadder. And this is the account of his journey that Ripley gave to Baer.

"I was at the captain's table the first night out and telling him how I wanted to find some of the Mayan ruins. 'I can put you in touch with just the man,' he told me. 'About ten years ago I was lying off the coast of Honduras and a small launch came alongside with a couple of men in it. One of them was a political refugee and he asked for asylum with me. I naturally gave it to him. But before it came time for us to leave, another large craft hove to and demanded the surrender of the refugee. When I refused, they tied up and boarded us. I drove them off with water hoses—we were not armed. And on the way back up the coast I dropped him at Havana. Now he is back in his homeland and operating a large sisal hemp plantation inland. It is difficult to get to him, but it will be worth your time and trouble, I assure you.'

"Well, naturally, I took his advice. And when we put into port I telephoned Blackadder's friend. He was most kind and sent a car for me—it was twenty-five miles or so over some pretty rough roads, but the man was very knowledgeable about the area. He gave me a lot of good steers and a couple of letters to government authorities that later helped open some doors for me.

"We had been talking about three hours and getting along just swell. It was late afternoon, and one of the servants had pulled the blinds to keep out the slanting rays of the sun. We were sitting in a very big barnlike reception room—a two-storied affair, with a sort of balcony along one end—having some drinks. And then this man says to me, 'Señor Ripley, as you may know, we have different customs here and we do not parade our womenfolk. But you and I have become friends in this short time and I would like you to meet her; especially because she too is a North American and I know it would be a great pleasure for her.' I said I'd be just delighted and he went off to call her upstairs.

"I was facing the balcony and I saw this woman walking along it and the one thing I could tell from where I was was that she was a real Junoesque type. She was wearing a long gown that came down to the floor. She started down the flight of stairs, and she was very graceful. I rose as she got near the bottom and walked over to meet her. The light was very poor and it was kind of shadowy, but when I got about fifteen feet from her I began to get a very strange feeling, and I really felt kind of clammy all of a sudden, although I didn't know why for a second or two.

"Then it hit me. This guy's wife was Doris.

"I gotta say that she carried it off much better than I did.

"'It is indeed a great pleasure to meet you, Señor Ripley,' she said very graciously. There was no outward trace of recognition. Then she smiled just a little and added, 'I have heard and read so very much about you.' We just sat there, talking and drinking for about an hour, and there wasn't anything at all between us that would have told her husband anything. I did cut short the visit, though, because it was a little creepy. I was supposed to stay for dinner but told them I was eager to get started and look for those old ruins.

"As I got into the car, Doris was at the door, and the last thing I saw was her framed in the doorway, waving, but very discreetly. Bugs, you can Believe That or Not."

Rip told me the same startling tale, but the locale was Saudi Arabia and Doris was the wife of a sheik. In this version—and there were probably others—he was not sure the woman he met was the one who had once been his mistress until he returned to his hotel (he was a bit vague about where it was) and found a note from her reading, "Roy, you'll always be the only one I love."

"Who else in that part of the world called me 'Roy?'" he would demand, if the story met with skeptical looks.

CHAPTER IV

On the Job

BOB achieved a certain poetic perfection of "Believe It or Not" on the day in 1927 when he introduced Albert J. Smith to the world. Albert lived in Dedham, Massachusetts. He was a one-armed paper hanger. And he suffered from the hives.

The Albert Smith cartoon was a perfect "Believe It or Not," by Ripley standards, because it was bizarre, contained a "shock of discovery" sure to arouse the reader, and lent itself to effective illustration. Obviously Rip could not hope to match this combination day in and day out, but practically all the thousands of BIONs he drew over the years contained at least one of the elements. The range of facts that he dished up at the rate of four to seven a day in his feature is well displayed in a "Ripley sampler" he put together as a guest column for Walter Winchell.

BY ROBERT L. RIPLEY.
Believe It or Not, Walter!

A baseball team can make one double, 2 singles, 3 triples and steal 2 bases—all in one inning—without scoring a run.

✿　✿　✿

Queen Anne gave birth to 17 children, but she died without an heir.

* * *

A hen owned by Neal Murray, Sanford, Maine, lays empty eggs.

* * *

Baked ice is a favorite Chinese dish. Try it. Roll a piece of ice in flour, put it on a fire, and eat it—but quickly.

* * *

A man once married a statue. Lord Orserey fell in love with the Venus de Medici and legally married it. He gave the statue a ring costing $100,000.

* * *

A coin the size of a nickel made of star matter would weigh 200 lbs.

* * *

Byron Gilbert, of Atchison, Kansas, when only seven years old, successfully passed a rigid examination before Supreme Court Justices and became a lawyer. He lives in Chicago now.

* * *

Thomas MacClure, of Detroit, hypnotizes fish.

* * *

Jack Spiro, a lawyer, can spell backward as fast as you can spell forward.

* * *

The word noise in Japanese is written with three characters representing women.

* * *

A bundle of spider webs no larger than a pea, if untangled and straightened out, would reach 350 miles.

❖   ❖   ❖

A ship weighs less going east than going west.

❖   ❖   ❖

It is possible for a person to live in three centuries and not be 100 years old.

❖   ❖   ❖

Charlemagne sat on his throne for 351 years.

❖   ❖   ❖

It takes two years to make a billiard ball.

❖   ❖   ❖

ROTTEN ROW is one of the most desirable places in London.

❖   ❖   ❖

LAST WILL AND TESTAMENT: First—I leave and bequeath to my first son John Ling, the sum of one dollar. With the said sum it is my wish that he purchase a rope strong and long enough to support his Irish wife.

❖   ❖   ❖

L. R. Chippel of Grand Rapids, Michigan, drove his car 185,000 miles without denting a fender.

❖   ❖   ❖

Napoleon conferred the Legion of Honor on a retreating soldier.

❖   ❖   ❖

C. Rioux bowled 302 without making a perfect score.

*   *   *

Charlie Peterson ran 100 points at straight rail billiards in 26 minutes.

*   *   *

W. Shott, of Cleveland, pitched a nine-inning game without allowing a hit, or a walk, or a man to reach first, and his team made no errors—yet he lost—1–0.

*   *   *

Stonewall Jackson, the great Confederate general, was killed by his own men—by his own orders.

*   *   *

Mrs. James Howard Booth, of Hammond, Ind., did not take a drink of water in 84 years. She lived 100 years.

*   *   *

Henry Morgenthau is not Treasurer of the United States.

*   *   *

Samuel Peas, of San Francisco, dined alone at Solari's Grill every night for 21 years.

*   *   *

Mozart wrote his own requiem on his own deathbed.

*   *   *

ENG and CHANG, original Siamese twins, were bitter enemies and at one time did not speak to each other for 3 years. CHANG was of noble birth and ENG was a Commoner and both died at the age of 70.

*   *   *

Johnny "Cigars" Connors, of Roxbury, Mass., rolled a peanut with his nose from Boston to Worcester.

✿ ✿ ✿

There are green clouds in Australia.

✿ ✿ ✿

There is a place in the world where all clocks are correct, whether they run fast, or don't run at all.

✿ ✿ ✿

The aroma of a dish of baked beans was the annual rent paid for the Cathedral of Cologne for 400 years.

✿ ✿ ✿

Carrie Nation played more ball games than Ty Cobb.

✿ ✿ ✿

Old man River is a woman—Mrs. Sippi.

✿ ✿ ✿

John Paul Jones, U. S. Naval Hero, was not an American citizen, did not command a fleet of American ships and his name was not Jones.

Sports items like those in the above compilation always figured importantly in "Believe It or Not." Ripley's early cartoons consisted entirely of sports oddities, or little-known records, such as the fact that Jimmy Johnston stole 124 bases in 1913 while playing with the San Francisco Seals in the Pacific Coast League, or that Andy Bowen and Jack Burke boxed 110 rounds at the Olympic Club in New Orleans in

1893 and that the referee stopped the fight and called it "no contest."

This preference of the artist for sports oddities was understandable, since his entire newspaper background had been in sports and he had been a better-than-average athlete himself during his Santa Rosa boyhood. Thus he knew about the thousands of athletic oddities lying in dusty record books, available to a diligent researcher. Quite a number of Rip's sports items wouldn't be found in most sports record books, however. A classic example of the latter was a cartoon showing Babe Ruth at the completion of a swing with the startling caption—"Babe Ruth Hit 125 Home Runs in One Hour."

Since this appeared months before the Babe had hit his record breaking sixty in the American League—a record which still stands—the uproar it provoked was gratifying to Ripley. His explanation was simplicity itself: Ruth had appeared in an exhibition baseball game at Wrigley Field, Los Angeles, in February 1927, and stood at home plate for an hour, during which time a series of pitchers threw to him, throwing with the sole idea of getting the ball over the plate. In that time, the Babe knocked 125 drives over the fence.

It is a matter of conjecture whether the enthusiasm of the public for Ripley's form of art, which was demonstrably high, was any greater than Bob's own enthusiasm for it. It became his be-all-and-end-all. A close friend once described Ripley's mania for the unusual this way:

"You go into a restaurant with Rip and you both order sirloin steaks," said the friend. "While you're waiting to be served, if you think about the steak at all, you wonder whether it will be properly cooked, too small or too big, something along those lines. Not so with Ripley. He's probably figuring how many steaks there are in a full-grown steer, how many steers there are in the state of Texas. Then he'll come up with a statement that there are enough steaks in Texas to feed the entire population of the Gaspé Peninsula for eighteen and a half years, three times a day.

"Of course," added the friend, "how to get the steaks from Texas to the Gaspé Peninsula, who is going to pay for them, or whether the people up there might not grow tired of steak three times a day after a couple of years, wouldn't enter into Bob's calculations. All he is interested in is coming up with a startling statement for his damned 'Believe It or Not.' The thing is more than an obsession with him; it's a complete way of life. He's not merely riding the gravy train—he's the engineer as well!"

Although Ripley found his proper niche in the creative world by accident, he developed it through application and intelligence. The late William Bolitho, writing in *Camera Obscura* about Ripley, observed that he had "the curiosity of the unlearned." It is true that Ripley developed what might be termed an unusual approach to the unusual. Thus, it would not be enough to inform Ripley that there was a two-headed calf in Shamokin, Pennsylvania. He would want the monstrosity to have other stigmata, such as coloring on its flanks that suggested an outline map of the United States.

Somewhere along the line Ripley developed what he was pleased to call "shockers." Since his professional reputation depended upon his ability to jog the reader into wakefulness, these proved extremely successful. Bob tried to outrage the reader by presenting a new twist to the commonplace or by making a bald denial of something which had been accepted for generations as true.

A perfect example was the statement that "George Washington was *not* the first President of the United States." It developed that John Hanson, when he signed the Articles of Confederation as a representative of Maryland, was elected

"President of the United States in Congress Assembled," 1781. Ripley's technique was to make the statement first and then produce the proof. If the reader felt that he had been had, Ripley's satisfaction was all the greater. He was the only man who delighted in being called a liar. Indeed, he claimed to have been called a liar more often than anyone else in the world. Far from being affronted, Bob accepted this as testimony of the success of his cartoons.

Three of Ripley's "shockers" are among the best known of their kind. They reveal Bob's true ingenuity, his ability to twist circumstances, to read oddities into commonplace situations. His "The Marching Chinese" is one of the most famous. The picture showed an endless string of Chinese, wearing coolie hats and marching four abreast, seemingly around the globe.

Ripley captioned it "The Marching Chinese" and wrote under it: "If all the Chinese in the world were to march—4 abreast—past a given point they would never finish passing, though they marched forever and ever." To prove his point in this case, Ripley used figures taken from a census of China in 1402 and 1403, indicating that the population gained nineteen per cent in a year. These were the last years a census had been taken in China, and Ripley, making his own rule-of-thumb vital statistics for a country where no such figures had been compiled in more than five centuries, decided there were six hundred million Chinese on earth. Arbitrarily setting his own birth rate and death rate for the Chinese, he figured that the population was increased at the rate of thirty million a year. War, famine, flood, and pestilence Ripley simply threw out the window. Taking U. S. Army marching regulations—three miles an hour and fifteen miles a day—the artist calculated that it would take 22 years and 302 days for the six hundred million Chinese to pass a given point. That would be time enough for a new generation. Ripley figured 26,280,000 passing the given point each year while thirty million were being born and surviving to replace them.

The ingenuity Ripley used to prove the point, at least to his own satisfaction, is a measure of the man. He dealt in the incredible, and therefore believed nothing was impossible. In his explanation, while citing the U. S. Army field regulations on marching, Ripley settled for fifteen miles a day, which would consume only five hours of the twenty-four. This point he blithely ignored in his explanation.

When Charles A. Lindbergh flew solo from Roosevelt Field, Long Island, to Le Bourget in Paris in early 1927, he captivated the imagination of the world. He particularly captivated the imagination of Ripley. Bob, as usual, thought of any achievement only in terms of material for his daily "Believe It or Not."

Ripley had by this time moved his drawing board from the *Globe* to the *Post*—the former sheet had died in 1923—a fact which the switchboard operators of that journal had cause to regret when the cartoonist finally found a way to exploit Lindbergh's feat. Bob drew an excellent picture of Lindbergh's Ryan monoplane flying through the clouds of the night over the Atlantic and captioned it: "Lindbergh Was the 67th Man to Make a Non-Stop Flight Over the Atlantic Ocean." The reaction startled even Ripley, who, like the Chinese of whom he was so fond, had a great capacity for not being surprised.

The switchboards at the *Post* lit up with a brilliance New York publishing had never known. Telegrams and letters poured in. Again Ripley confounded his accusers with a simple explanation, one which no doubt outraged many of them. He pointed out that he hadn't denied Lindbergh was the first to fly *solo* nonstop across the Atlantic, merely that he wasn't the first to fly nonstop. Then Bob cited Sir John Alcock and Sir A. Whitton Brown, who made the first nonstop flight across the Atlantic, from Newfoundland to Ireland, in 1919. In that same year, an English dirigible, the *R-34*, crossed from Scotland to America and returned, with a crew of thirty-one men; and in 1924 a German Zeppelin (*ZR-3*, later to become the ill-fated *Los Angeles*) crossed from Friedrichshafen, Germany, to Lakehurst, New Jersey, with a crew of thirty-three.

According to Ripley's arithmetic, and Ripley's logic, all this made Lindbergh the sixty-seventh man to fly nonstop across the Atlantic. The defense rested, while Bob gleefully tabulated the 170,000 letters his Lindbergh cartoon attracted.

Ripley was an intense patriot. He declared, via a cartoon, that America had no national anthem; that Francis Scott Key, writing the words to "The Star-Spangled Banner" in besieged Fort McHenry in Baltimore harbor in 1812, had later set them to the music of an English drinking song.

The cartoonist was on solid ground here. Key had indeed taken the music from a tavern ballad he had discovered in a songbook of the time. Furthermore, the song never had been adopted as the official anthem of the United States. Inundated by another flood of mail, Bob called for help. "Don't write to me; write to your Congressman," was his plea. More than five million people did write to their representatives in Washington, and two years after the cartoon appeared, "The Star-Spangled Banner" was officially adopted as the national anthem, almost a hundred and twenty years after it had been written.

Much as Ripley delighted in coming up with mail-producing "shockers" such as his "Marching Chinese," Lindbergh's ranking as a nonstop transatlantic aeronaut, or the nation's failure formally to adopt a national anthem, he was happy, too, when he could stick his readers on a technicality. Folklore was a big help to him when he ventured onto these tangents. He did an excellent portrait of William F. Cody, known to millions as "Buffalo Bill." Underneath this picture of the mighty hunter, resplendent in his buckskin trappings, Ripley wrote: "Buffalo Bill Never Shot a Buffalo in His Life." Bob's "out" in this case was that the animal which Cody slew by the dozens was a bison, not a buffalo.

Ripley once drove the nation's golfers—including the professionals—stark, raving mad, with the statement that it was possible to drive a golf ball *uphill* two miles with a single stroke. "Simple," said Bob when stormed for an explanation. All you had to do was find a straight stretch of frozen river two miles long. Tee up the ball, smack it, and it would roll interminably on the ice, since ice produces a minimum of friction. As to driving the ball *uphill* for the two miles, Ripley explained that hitting *upstream* was the same as hitting *uphill*. It wasn't one of Ripley's better explanations, for Bob never did locate a river possessing these qualifications, let alone one which, when frozen over, would have a glassily smooth surface for a two-mile stretch. His explanation satisfied Ripley, however, which was all he ever asked.

Some of "Ripley's Believe It or Not" rested on rather flimsy evidence, such as: "The surgeon Dr. Politman, a native of Lorraine, died at the age of 140, having been drunk each day since he was 25 years old. On the eve of his death he performed a major surgical operation successfully." For the authenticity of this, Bob rested his case entirely on a story by a Dr. W. Rullman, which ran in two installments in the *Vossische Zeitung* of Berlin in March 1916.

There was no verification of the alcoholic surgeon's age, the period in which he lived, drank, and died, or even the location of his practice. It is an insight into Ripley's obsession, his search for the curious, that he accepted anything in print as authentic. It wasn't that Bob didn't know better; it was simply one of the rules he adopted for the game—*his* game. As long as he could cite an authority for something he printed, he felt he was off the hook, regardless of how feeble the authority might be, on investigation.

Ripley had dozens of paid assistants, researchers, and so on, but he also had thousands and thousands of unpaid assistants. Many of the letters he received contained odd facts which found their way onto his drawing board, but only after they had been "authenticated."

A correspondent once wrote that a certain Señor Lascurain had served for thirty-seven minutes as President of Mexico before being removed from office through the "lead impeachment" popular in so many countries around the turn of the century. Ripley, of course, was fascinated by the statement, but, according to the rules, he had to find a printed verification. His research staff was dispatched, en masse, to the New York Public Library to search through all the books which dealt with, or even mentioned, the Mexican revolution of 1913.

"They found the reference they were seeking in the 9832d book," Bob proudly told an interviewer. He neglected to authenticate that statement, nor did he ever reveal who counted the books his researchers pored through. Nevertheless, Lascurain made "Believe It or Not"—an honor which, in Ripley's mind, was at least equal to enshrinement in the pantheon of the gods.

As Ripley's financial base broadened with Hearst, he set up a sort of global bird-dog posse to hunt down international oddities. Through Joe Connolly, who was indubitably the man behind Ripley's newspaper successes, Bob had a standing order with International News Service "stringers" around the world to forward any likely-looking tidbits. Any of these

items which could be used as "Believe It or Not" material
was worth $50 to the "stringer" who excavated it. These were
the only pieces of material for his cartoons for which Ripley
ever paid any money.

A "stringer," in press-association usage, is a part-time em-
ployee, paid a small weekly retainer (far less than the $50
Ripley offered) to be available to assist the regular corre-
spondents when a story breaks in his territory. The "stringer"
is then paid an additional sum, in proportion to the assistance
he renders the salaried correspondent in his territory. It is
possible that these "stringers" took advantage of Ripley with
an occasional planted story. A man of imagination could whip
up an item with the date line of an obscure (or even imagi-
nary) hamlet in Central Europe and see that it was printed in
a newspaper. Ripley was constantly being informed of people
who led healthy lives past the century mark, of girls who
became mothers before they were ten. This was all grist for
the Ripley mill—as long as Bob had the printed documentation to go along with it.

The truth was that Ripley literally believed everything. He
made flat statements such as "Neils Paulsen, of Uppsala, Swe-
den, died in 1907 at the age of 160 and left two sons—one
nine years old and the other 103 years of age." His sources
were usually reprints of old newspapers for items such as the
long-lived Swede—rarely medical records, birth certificates,
or such. All Ripley's extensive travels were a search for oddities. He once made a trip to Vienna because someone told him
of the legend behind the famed song "Ach, du lieber Augustine." He learned that the song was said to have been first
sung by a man named Augustine, who had fallen into a
drunken stupor in one of the Viennese streets when that city
had been struck by bubonic plague.

To prevent the spread of the plague, bodies were buried

in a mass grave in the city. The drunken Augustine, lying unconscious in the street, was assumed to be a plague victim and was tossed in a collecting cart with the corpses of victims. He came to in the mass grave (called the *Graben*, to this day) and began to sing out drunken songs, which saved him from being buried with the corpses. Thus was the song created. Ripley found the anecdote delightful. The story is famous in Europe, of course, but by journeying all the way to Vienna to "discover" it, Bob could introduce it more dramatically in the United States.

On another tour, Ripley made a special trip to San Blas, an archipelago off the northeast coast of Panama, because he had been told that primitive Indians there had a unique method of celebrating Christmas Day. Bob found that the feast was celebrated with a succession of cockfights. Considering that cockfights were staged on practically all holidays and Sundays in that section of Panama, the trip was hardly rewarding, but Rip never complained. It was a place which he hadn't been to before, and Bob considered any place he hadn't been well worth seeing, regardless of its scenic or historic qualifications. It also was the two hundredth country he had visited, according to his own calculations.

Ripley also drew a cartoon depicting one of the locks of the Panama Canal, and the text said, "A postage stamp built the Panama Canal." This was one of his more involved explanatory efforts, and its authentication was so complex that Bob eventually built an entire radio show from it. The French had obtained rights to build a canal across the Isthmus of Panama in 1878, but it was an abortive effort which dragged along for years and finally bogged down completely in one of those widespread scandals so peculiar to French syndicates. A young engineer, Philippe Jean Bunau-Varilla, alone remained enthusiastic. When he failed to get any encouragement, or money, from his own people, he came to Washington to interest the Americans. There had been, of course, talk of a canal through Central America for decades, but no definite decision had been reached.

The United States by this time had just about decided upon routing the canal—which would eliminate the long voyage around Cape Horn—through Nicaragua, not Panama. Nicaragua had one of the largest lakes in the Western Hemisphere, Lake Nicaragua, and by utilizing this lake as part of the waterway, construction costs could be cut enormously. A bill to vote funds for a canal to go through Nicaragua was slated to come before Congress.

Bunau-Varilla promptly became a one-man lobby. He obtained several hundred Nicaraguan postage stamps, which showed a picture of one of the country's small volcanoes in full eruption. Bunau-Varilla wrote a brief letter to each Congressman, asking, in effect, if it were really wise to build a canal—at great cost to the American taxpayers—through a country which was filled with active volcanoes. With each letter went one of the Nicaraguan stamps. The Congressmen read the letter, looked at the stamp, and decided not to vote funds for a canal through Nicaragua.

It was two years later (1904) before Congress bought the uncompleted Panamanian waterway from the French and ten years longer before the Panama Canal was completed, but, as far as Ripley was concerned, "A postage stamp built the Panama Canal."

As Ripley's fame increased, so, of course, did his imitators and his critics. Although Bob was as unpolished a businessman as you would find in a day's travel by jet, he (or perhaps his editors) had the good sense to obtain a copyright on the title "Believe It or Not." The phrase was so closely associated, not only with Ripley, but with his type of feature, that his imitators were forced into devising some strange titles for their own work. One enterprising chap took a stab at "Believe It or Don't," but the courts promptly set upon him. Another title was "You Don't Tell Me——."

Many of Ripley's critics and/or imitators thought of Bob as a charlatan. They disputed his authentications, some of which, as has been seen, were based on rather flimsy evidence. Yet they missed the point entirely. Rip was, first of all, a superb artist, and he possessed a larger bump of curiosity and a livelier mind than any of his imitators. His was a mind uncluttered by culture, which meant that everything was new to him, including the respective ages of Cleopatra and Mark Antony when they met by the Nile or the fact that William Shakespeare spelled his name differently from time to time. These were things anybody with a fair secondary-school education could have told Ripley—and probably did. Yet it was upon such facts as these that he built his cartoons, his fame, and his wealth.

Few things delighted Ripley more than the opportunity to combine a challenging statement with a full-scale drawing, as he did with Lindbergh's solo flight across the Atlantic. When Rip stumbled on the fact that the Battle of Waterloo did not confine itself to that village but was fought over the surrounding territory, at Mont-Saint-Jean, Belle-Alliance, and other places, he did a magnificent black and white drawing of Napoleon in retreat from the field, surrounded by men fleeing on horse and foot, with supply wagons, tattered standards and broken drums, with the smoke of battle hanging over all. It is captioned "The Battle of Waterloo was *not* fought at Waterloo."

Ripley, for his documentation, quoted Victor Hugo in *Les Misérables* when he made the observation, ". . . and Waterloo, which had no share in the battle, has all the honor." Incidentally, in citing this reference, Ripley ignored Hugo as a poet, novelist, and dramatist and referred to him only as "a great authority on the Napoleonic era."

From time to time, Ripley took dead aim on axioms. "A straight line is not the shortest distance between two points," he proclaimed one day in his feature. Then he added, "Lindbergh proved that when he flew from New York to Paris. Lindy flew what is known as an 'arc of the great circle.'" He also obtained considerable mileage from such truisms as "There is no lead in a lead pencil—it is graphite," and "a cuttle fish is not a fish—it is an octopus." Obviously such misnomers, so to speak, offered a fertile field and one which Rip plowed nearly barren.

It always was Ripley's contention that there was no end to the "Believe It or Not." "The supply is inexhaustible. Each day it becomes easier to obtain," he once wrote in a preface to one of his books. It all depended, of course, on the point of view as to what constituted an authentic "Believe It or Not." And, since it was Ripley who created the feature, his point of view was the only one that mattered.

Words fascinated Ripley. One of his cartoons contained the word "ambidextrously" with the profound observation that this word contained fourteen letters, not a single one of which was repeated. Palindromes constituted another wellspring which Bob tapped frequently, running all the way from, "Madam, I'm Adam," and "Able was I Ere I Saw Elba," to, "A War at Tarawa," "Pa's a Sap." The last Ripley amplified with the statement, "Pa's a sap, no matter how you look at it."

Although Ripley never in his life was able to balance a checkbook, he relied heavily on mathematics for his features, particularly permutations such as one which carried pi from its usual 3.14159 to 707 decimal places! He also noted that the number 2520 was divisible by all the digits from one to nine and inquired, "How many do you know that are?"

A statement of Ripley's that it was possible for an average adult to jump through a hole in a cigarette paper attracted considerable mail, including one from the Infanta Beatriz, daughter of ex-King Alfonso. Ripley then printed a diagram showing how the cigarette paper could be cut—theoretically, at least—to be opened into a wide enough circle for a person to jump through. It involved forty-four cuts through the paper across its width and one through its length. Obviously so many incisions in so tiny and fragile a surface would call for someone as highly skilled as a surgeon. Ripley, when printing the diagrammed explanation, gratuitously warned his readers to be careful not to tear the paper!

Certainly many of Ripley's features, such as jumping through a hole in a cigarette paper, had a touch of charlatanism to them, but none of this ever affected the popularity of his cartoons. It was a parlor game with his readers. They would use his outrageous statements as a conversation piece and then supply Ripley's answer. It would have surprised Bob to find that there were people who could be hoaxed by his tricks, since he assumed *everybody* read him.

As remarkable as any subject Ripley ever presented was the fact that in the last thirty years of his lifetime no paper ever canceled the feature. It was understandable that Bob's work became an obsession with him. Dr. Wilfred Funk, the famed lexicographer, was reported to have tentatively created a new adjective to describe Ripley's work. The work was Ripleiadian, a combination of "Ripley" and "pleiad," meaning a cluster of brilliant things.

Ripley turned out a prodigious amount of work. He was supposed to keep from three to ten weeks ahead on his newspaper cartoons, but didn't. So when the backlog began to dip, and he was being prodded by Bradley Kelly, comic-art editor of King Features, he thought nothing of getting up at 6:00 A.M. and working the day through, turning out a week or two of features during the session. Usually Bob went to his drawing board early in the morning, clad only in sandals and a bathrobe which looked ancient enough to have served as an imperial toga for Nero. He drew his cartoons upside-down with a stub pen. He used only printed block letters, this habit extending even to his somewhat meager correspondence, whenever he got around to answering a letter, which was not often.

As Ripley's income mounted so that he could hire a staff of researchers, he also allowed himself the luxury of assistant artists, usually young fellows who would letter in the work after the master had composed it. Sometimes, when Bob was feeling particularly lazy or hung-over, his assistants were permitted to complete the cartoon, with shading, after he had outlined it. But to the end his cartoons always bore the unmistakable stamp of Ripley.

CHAPTER V

Ripley and the Men in Gray

NOT since Ulysses Simpson Grant and William Tecumseh Sherman had the men in gray been so harassed by an individual as mailmen were by Bob Ripley. No person—president or king, potentate or dictator—consistently received more mail than Ripley.

Figures, unless they're in the front line of a musical, tend to be boring, but the influx of mail to Ripley can't be truly appreciated unless some examples are cited. A continuous-line puzzle which he ran in his "Believe It or Not" cartoon brought in 207,000 requests for the solution. A cartoon question—"What is the shortest verse in the Bible?"—drew answers from 32,000 women alone. The shortest verse in the Bible, incidentally, is "Jesus wept" (John 10:35).

It was when Ripley went heavily into contests, however, in the early 1930s that he finally had the letter carriers humpbacked and bowlegged under the weight of their sacks. A two-week contest which Ripley ran nationally in 104 daily newspapers—offering prizes for the best "Believe It or Nots" submitted—drew 1,750,000 entry letters. In a contest conducted over only six New England radio stations, more than 50,000 persons sent in entry blanks. A two-week contest in 66 newspapers resulted in 895,000 entries.

Letters are the bread and butter of any columnist conducting a feature because they provide a rough measure of reader interest, but it is doubtful if anyone ever greeted his mail with the enthusiasm Ripley did. This zeal did not extend to his answering it, of course, for Bob was notorious as a poor correspondent, even with his closest friends. Napoleon is credited with the delayed system of handling correspondence. It was the emperor's custom to let letters go two weeks without answering them. "By that time," Bonaparte is supposed to have said, "you'd be surprised how many of them require no answer." Ripley went the emperor one better. He allowed the letters to go a couple of months without even opening them.

Ripley's mail bolstered his ego. The volume of it fascinated him. So did the character of it.

A letter written on the back of a Japanese postage stamp and addressed simply, "Ripley, North America," was delivered to his New York office without unusual delay. It was sent by Francis Arnold of the American Legation in Peking and mailed from Yokohama. The fact that such a unique message could reach him titillated Bob to such an extent that he used it in one of his cartoons.

Bob's fans, who were as unusual as they were numerous, promptly wrote messages addressed to him on the backs of ordinary United States postage stamps, dropped them in the mailboxes, and they were delivered.

The one cartoon produced a veritable avalanche of curiously addressed letters to Ripley. Some contained no writing on the envelope at all, simply a tear on the front of the envelope to indicate "Rip." There were letters whose sole address was a ripply line or series of such lines. Letters were received with nothing on the envelope but a scrawled question mark.

Ripley dutifully reprinted in his cartoon feature the more unusual of the freakishly addressed letters. Now it seemed his readers wanted to outdo each other in tricky addressing. Hundreds came in with nothing but a photograph of Ripley pasted on the outside. A penny postcard was received which bore only this phrase, ". . . I was waiting for a street car!"

Letters were received from all parts of the world, addressed in all languages and dialects, including one in English, which was captioned only, "To the Biggest Liar in the World." Now Bob's readers had a chance to prove they were as ingenious as he. Letters came to him in Boy Scout semaphore, shorthand, Navy wigwag, dactylology, a Confederate Civil War code, Indian signs, and the Morse code.

When the Ripley followers ran out of curious ways of addressing their letters, they turned to using objects other than paper—woods and metals, rocks, eggs, and bones of animals. In his *Believe It or Not Omnibus*, Ripley recorded receiving a letter written on a grain of rice by E. I. Blystone of Ardara, Pennsylvania. The grain of rice was mailed in an ordinary envelope, which had no name or address, only a picture of a bird drawn in flourishing lines. A microscopic examination revealed that the lines contained the name "Robert Ripley" written thirty-five hundred times.

It also, of course, required a microscope to read the message written on the grain of rice. "It [the message] contained 1615 letters," wrote Ripley, "which means that Mr. Blystone had written eight ordinary typewritten pages on this minute space." This was a Ripley misstatement. An ordinary page of typewriter paper (8½ x 11) has room on it, double-spaced, for thirty lines of sixty letters each, or eighteen hundred letters. Rip might have confused letters and words.

All this trick mail added up to shrewd promotion on Ripley's part. Every columnist is delighted by mail, but only Rip could draw such curious mail. The Japanese stamp, mailed from Yokohama by Mr. Arnold of the American Legation in Peking, could have been a one-shot thing if Rip had not capitalized on it. Again this is where Ripley's detractors underrate the man.

He knew from his correspondence that, among the millions who followed his feature, there were thousands whose mental processes ran along the same bizarre lines as his own.

The bald truth is that the Ripley feature was as unusual as the facts depicted in it. The hard core of the followers of "Believe It or Not" found it both stimulating and provocative.

To this inner circle of Ripley *aficionados* the trickily addressed letters were a challenge, and one which was accepted as such. The more ingeniously addressed letters were published in Rip's daily feature, goading other fans to surpass them. For the purposes of authentication, the artist wisely preserved the originals and they later were placed on display in the Fourth Avenue offices of his publishers.

Not even the U.S. government could alter the flow or nature of Ripley's correspondence. On April 19, 1930, after the first few torrents of peculiarly addressed mail, Postmaster General Walter F. Brown issued a directive to postal employees which read, in part:

> ". . . Such letters hereafter will be either returned to the sender or sent to the Dead Letter Office. Postal clerks have had to devote too much time recently to deciphering freak letters intended for Ripley."

It seems, however, that Rip had his admirers among the postal clerks too. When Brown's directive was published in the newspapers, a stamp company in Baltimore, Maryland, pasted the clipping on the outside of a stamped, but otherwise blank, envelope and dropped it in the mailbox. It reached Ripley promptly at King Features.

The great mass of mail which reached Ripley's office daily was, of course, winnowed by a staff of clerks. Those which seemed to have suggestions worth cartoon material were placed in one batch; letters which seemed to require the master's personal attention were placed in another; and the fan mail was handled by form replies of acknowledgment. Some of Rip's readers had rather weird ideas of what constituted "Believe It or Not" material. One correspondent offered to authenticate the story of a visiting spinster who stuck to a newly varnished toilet seat. The family doctor, called to extricate the maiden lady, was convulsed with laughter, fell against the bathtub, breaking two ribs. An ambulance was summoned to take physician, spinster, and toilet seat to the hospital.

"I can give you the names, dates, and hospital records," offered this eager beaver. It was Ripley's opinion that it was much better left untold.

Ripley's many secretaries found his personal correspondence a problem. He could neither be cajoled nor bullied into answering it. "Put it aside, put it aside," he rasped impatiently. "I'll decide what to say later." No matter how often the secretaries protested that the stack of mail "put aside" was growing, Rip never budged. Even letters from close friends were thus treated. It reached the point where the secretaries felt duty-bound to telephone some of Bob's nearest and dearest and explain that the letters had been received, that Bob had seen them, and that they would be answered—maybe.

The only time Ripley showed a twinge of conscience about his correspondence was when he was on the eve of taking off for some remote spot such as Tanganyika or Hong Kong. Then he would stuff handfuls of it into an already crammed valise, with the avowed intention of answering it while globe hopping. Actually, Bob had less time to answer mail while traveling than at home, but it was a fiction he maintained to the end.

Ripley's habit of carrying his mail with him led to one of the most unusual events in his life, which was studded

with the unusual. Once, while flying over the desert to Lake
Chad in French West Africa, Bob actually took out a packet
of, not only unanswered, but unopened, letters. Whether he
intended answering them or merely reading them nobody will
ever know. He grew bored after gazing at one or two and
flung the entire batch out of the sliding plane window.

The letters, still bound in thick elastic bands, were found in
the desert by a band of wandering nomads. Literate or not,
they knew mail when they saw it and took the packet to the
nearest oasis or village and turned it over to somebody in
authority. The letters beat Ripley back to New York. Ripley
was as delighted as a schoolboy valedictorian when he returned home and heard the full story. His enthusiasm, however, did not extend to his reopening the packet.

Ripley's refusal to keep abreast of his correspondence
stemmed not from rudeness but rather from a combination of
boredom and impatience. Bob was eager to find out what was
happening now, or what was going to happen next, not what
had happened already. He preserved the same attitude toward business documents, allowing contracts to lie around,
unread and unsigned, for weeks.

Sometimes, but only rarely, Ripley would enter into an exchange of letters if his curiosity were sufficiently piqued. A
friend invited Bob to visit him in town. "Drop by some afternoon and we'll have a spot of tiffin," said his friend casually.

"You don't even know what tiffin means," snorted world
traveler Ripley. A friendly discussion followed, in which it
developed that neither was precisely sure of his ground.

To be unsure of anything, Ripley couldn't stand. He in-
vestigated the meaning of the word "tiffin." So did his friend.
The friend wrote that it originally was an Indian word, that
its first meaning was a drink but that later it came to mean
lunch.

This was one letter Ripley answered. "It's an old Northern English dialect word for a small draught of liquor," replied Bob. "When brought into India, it took on a new meaning, as a light lunch or snack. It is used almost exclusively by Anglo-Indians, but it is *not* an Indian word."

When the friend wrote again, this time to admit that Ripley's definition of the word was probably nearer the mark than his, Bob didn't bother to answer. He had proved his point and lost his interest.

Ripley's fascination with the mail he received offered another insight into his character. Still the essentially shy person who had walked to a New York publisher's office with his cartoons, lest he be lost in the catacombs of the then infant subway system, Ripley was thrilled by the fact that he had now become a sufficiently international celebrity to receive letters addressed in outlandish codes and rebuses. That he received more mail, by volume, than the President or anyone else in the world was a source of sheer enjoyment to him.

Answering mail, however, was a stamp of another color. Anybody could answer a letter, Ripley felt. The real achievement was in receiving it.

CHAPTER VI

Perfect Blend—Business and Pleasure

WORK, women, and travel were the primary ingredients in the life of Robert L. Ripley, and he managed to mix business and pleasure into what most men in their humdrum lives would regard as a perfect blend. It took some doing. When he was an inexperienced young man he approached vocation and avocation separately, although with ardor. Then he discovered that he could make travel pay off—by providing him with subject matter for his cartooning. When he finally hit the big money with his "Believe It or Not," and could afford those little extra conveniences not available in tourist class, he made it a point when traveling to include at least one attractive (preferably Oriental) woman with his drawing board, pith helmet, and other luggage.

After his first trip abroad, to Europe in 1914, Rip was kept close to home by World War I, limiting himself to short forays into Canada and Mexico. In 1920 he went to South America, and liked it so well that, when he had saved up enough money for another major foreign exploration, he went back for a second look. This was in 1924, and although Ripley would travel in much more lavish style later, he was never happier or more content.

Dick Hyman, who later served as Ripley's press agent and was his friend for a quarter of a century, was in Rio de Janeiro, Brazil, when Ripley arrived there in the fall of 1924.

Just out of prep school the previous June, Hyman had taken a freighter to South America, got off at Rio, and became co-editor of a weekly magazine, *The Brazilian American.*

Ripley, who had transferred by this time from the *Globe* to the New York *Post*, was combining business and pleasure on his trip. He was writing and drawing a special syndicated-column feature entitled "Rambles Round South America," in addition to "Believe It or Not." When he arrived in Rio he sought out "someone from home," an incurable American custom abroad, and was steered to Hyman. He explained that he'd like to go around the city and see what material he could gather for his column. Ripley impressed Hyman as friendly, shy in an appealing way, and primarily interested in his work. They toured the city and surrounding area together for several days.

One night Hyman brought an English-speaking Brazilian girl to dinner. It was no more than a casual date, and Hyman thought no more of it for several days—until he received an urgent cablegram from his father, begging Dick to think twice before marrying the girl! It seems that Ripley, in the syndicated column, had referred to her as Dick's fiancée and the elder Hyman had read the news in the Kansas City *Star.* For Hyman that was merely a taste of what life would be like when he was with Ripley.

Ripley was, then and later, a good traveler. He was physically strong—he often said that he got "the best gift parents can give a child, a strong body and sound health"—and he endured without complaint such discomforts as kidney-jarring rides over rough South American roads in pre-knee-action cars. Ripley also had almost total recall about any place he'd ever visited, so that as he traveled he was squirreling away facts that would serve him in later "Believe It or Nots."

In 1925 Ripley took his first trip to the Orient. He visited

Japan, China, Malaya, and the Philippines. Japan interested
him little (then or later), because the country was "getting
too modern," but seeing China for the first time was like "coming home"—to a land etched vividly for him in fact and fan-
tasy during his teen-age years in San Francisco. Not long
after this trip the cartoonist even signed some of his drawings
"Rip Li." He made this first trip to the Orient as a tourist-
class steamship passenger and was accompanied by a New
York newspaper pal, Bob Ellis. He returned to New York with
a stack of cartoons and hundreds of ideas for more "Believe
It or Nots."

Ripley didn't stay put long, and his next trip abroad was a
milestone in his life. Late in 1927 he went to Europe again,
and met "the only woman I ever really loved." He provided
this description some twenty years after the meeting—after
her death and when Rip himself was hopelessly addicted to
dramatic overstatement—but there is little doubt that among
the literally countless women who moved in and out of his
turbulent life he reserved a highly special place for the
woman he called "Oakie."

"Oakie" was a Russian refugee living in Paris when Ripley
visited there in 1927. She was a flashing-eyed Jewess, handsome, intelligent, and vital, a socially accomplished woman
who had a lot to offer the roughly finished Ripley. She joined
Rip as a combination social secretary and companion. Her
nickname came from her habit of saying, with the lingering
trace of a Russian accent, "Okie-dokie."

Oakie traveled around Europe in the Ripley entourage for
several months, introducing him to correct table manners,
getting him a bit more interested in serious art—although this
never really took—and generally making him a more socially
acceptable individual.

Over the years the women Rip truly admired were the in-

The *Mon-Lei* moored at the specially built dock on Lake Worth, Florida, at the foot of Ripley's beautiful estate.

In Germany, Ripley matches steins with a world's champion.

Ripley and a "holy man" sun gazer in India. This man vowed to stare at the sun forever, and of course became completely blind.

Ripley looking down on a "monkey man" in India. This "holy man" vowed never to walk upright, and could no longer stand erect.

Ripley with New Guinea head-hunters wearing tribal masks.

Ripley always posed a problem for the United States Customs. He is shown here, just back from a South American junket. UNITED PRESS INTERNATIONAL PHOTO

Kuda Bux, completely blindfolded by Bob Considine (right), joined the six-day bike race held in the Armory in 1949 and caused a sensation by making several turns. The feat was televised on Ripley's program.　　N.B.C. PHOTO

Ripley inspects a damaged naval gun on bombed-out Corregidor, shortly after World War II.

dependent ones. He might appear to favor those who were more submissive, but they rarely lasted long in his esteem, and he treated them like so much dirt underfoot; he would scream indignities at them and otherwise humiliate them. He would scream at Oakie, too, but she would scream right back, and almost invariably he would bow. Oakie, in fact, quickly earned the right to move in and out of Ripley's life as she pleased.

When Ripley returned to New York after that trip he left Oakie behind, but helped arrange for her to emigrate to the United States. She would later have to compete with other women—at home and abroad—but Oakie made that trip especially memorable for Ripley. It was the last one he took largely as an individual; thereafter his travel became more institutionalized and widely publicized. With Oakie that time he was carefree and happy.

Intensive promotion of Ripley as a "modern Marco Polo" started after he joined King Features Syndicate on July 9, 1929. This was partly Ripley's own idea—as shy as he was, he was also keenly aware of the publicity possibilities in anything he did—much of it stemmed from the promotion-minded Joe Connolly, and much from Dick Hyman, whom Rip hired in 1929 as his personal publicity representative.

Hyman's first assignment for Ripley had comparatively little to do with travel. Ripley was still living at the New York Athletic Club. His two-room suite there was comfortable, and he liked it, but one of the house rules was that no women were allowed above the main floor; Ripley's room number was 1801. So most of his assignations were scheduled at a hotel two blocks away, and Hyman was charged with taking a suitcase containing a Manhattan telephone directory (to give it weight, not for reading) into the hotel and registering Ripley in legally.

It was Hyman who was responsible for getting Ripley into an airplane for the first time—much against the latter's desire. Rip simply was afraid to fly and had resisted all blandishments. Hyman wasn't aware quite how fearful Rip was until he perpetrated a headline-making stunt when Ripley returned from a two-month tour of Europe and North Africa aboard the S.S. *Leviathan* in 1930. Ripley had not been warned in advance about the nature of the stunt.

Working in co-operation with the publicity department of the United States Lines, Hyman arranged to have the *Leviathan* stopped off Fire Island, some thirty miles outside New York City; a seaplane would pick Rip up there and deliver him to New York in time for a radio broadcast.

Hyman and his co-conspirators stayed up all night, watching weather reports, and in the morning, in a dense fog, two planes took off from Roosevelt Field. The first was a Stinson monoplane which contained reporters and still and newsreel photographers who were to witness the transfer of Rip to the amphibian. The amphibian itself was a four-place Loening, containing the pilot and Hyman.

The fog lifted just as the planes approached Fire Island and the amphibian put down in calm waters alongside the *Leviathan*. Passengers were lined up along the rails to witness the event, and as they did, a major drama of another type was under way in Ripley's cabin. It was the duty of the *Leviathan's* master, Captain Manning, to acquaint Ripley with the details of the stunt and to persuade him to come up on deck, get in a lifeboat, and permit the boat and himself to be lowered down to the waiting plane. Ripley finally complied, but he was reluctant and he was mad.

When he boarded the plane, Ripley would speak to no one. Sweating profusely, he glowered at Hyman but feigned indifference, studying a chart which he handled wrongside to.

The flight back was without incident, but Ripley was still in a black mood when the plane landed at Newark Airport. He spoke to no one, including the small welcoming committee at the airport, until he got back to the New York Athletic Club and saw early editions of the New York *Journal*. That paper carried banner headlines about Ripley's flight. His mood changed immediately. He became profusely grateful to Hyman. He beamed at everybody. And, forever after, he was sold on flying.

This was the most dramatic welcome arranged for Ripley, but in the ensuing years Connolly, Ripley himself, and others made sure that his comings and goings were widely noted. On several occasions there were triumphal dinners for him —most of them staged in benefit of some worthy organization —drawing crowds of up to fifteen hundred persons, including celebrities from every field. Connolly particularly dealt heavily in celebrities. In control of the mighty King Features Syndicate and, at one time, all the Hearst newspapers from coast to coast, Connolly could bring any publicity-conscious personality to heel. And he didn't hesitate to do so. This did not, of course, account for all the big names surrounding Ripley on these occasions of public celebration, for he numbered a great many celebrities among his friends.

In 1931, Rip was back in Europe and North Africa again. He was much more interested in the latter. Making on-the-spot sketches, he visited Moulay Idris, the ancient city of Morocco which all "infidels" (non-Moslems) had to leave before sundown. He went to Tripoli, and returned with a great many stories about this great stronghold of the Barbary Coast corsairs. He made a special point of going to Meknès to see the ruins of the great city once erected by one of the greatest of all family men, the Sultan Ismail, reputed to have fathered almost nine hundred children. He marveled at the old city

of Constantine, in Algeria, rising high above the deep gorge
of the Rhumel River, and deeply cut by ravines; Rip called
it "the city of the air" in "Believe It or Not." North Africa
on that and subsequent trips yielded a treasure trove of items
for Rip, and when he returned home, in June 1931, there was
also a dinner for five hundred friends at the Athletic Club.

By this time Rip was quite clearly a compulsive traveler,
a psychological quirk that he shared with, among others, an
individual as different as the German poet Rainer Maria Rilke.
He seemed to be on the move practically all the time now.
As with some others who shared his compulsion, he was restless and rootless, seeking something, he knew not what. And,
on a more mundane level, he also appeared to believe that he
was safest when he was on the move, a shifting target.

Among those aiming at him was a singer with whom he
had a tempestuous relationship. She was known to Rip and
his friends as a tartar—one of the few women who proved to
be tougher than Ripley himself. Hyman remembers that one
day she went to the New York Athletic Club, looking for Rip,
and when, after a long interval, he didn't come down from his
suite, she lay down on the floor of the lobby and screamed,
"I won't move until I get five hundred dollars from him!" Rip
sent the money down as soon as he was informed of her
demand.

Partly to avoid further incidents of this nature, Ripley was
soon off on what may have been the most glamorous and most
memorable of all his trips. Early in 1932, accompanied by a
lovely young woman, Ripley sailed aboard the de luxe liner
Mariposa. As befitted a man whose annual income was approaching the $500,000 mark—despite the depression—Ripley
traveled in great style. He had a veranda suite for himself
and his pretty little shipmate, and it would have been hard to
find greater luxury anywhere at that time.

In fact, this was sea travel at its most glamorous. The *Mariposa* was a brand-new member of the Matson Line fleet, a sister of the *Monterrey* and later the *Lurline*. It was a glistening white eighteen-thousand-ton two-stacker, bearing a giant yellow and blue letter "M" on one of the stacks. The crew was smartly turned out and well trained. There were fresh flowers on the dining-room tables and in the better suites. The two-room veranda suite that Rip occupied opened onto a ten-by-fifteen-foot private promenade looking out over the sea.

As luxurious as the *Mariposa* was, the food didn't come up to the standards of one of Ripley's shipmates on the voyage, Rudolf Friml, the noted Bohemian composer who was also a sybarite and gourmet of considerable scope. Friml thought the food was "barbaric," so when the ship put in at Sydney, Australia, Friml went ashore and returned with a leg of lamb, eggs, fresh vegetables, spices, and assorted goodies. He had the lamb prepared by the ship's cook, under his direction, exactly as he wanted it—stuffed with garlic—and brought to the dining table with appropriate ceremonial. They all had a feast.

It was while the ship was docked in Sydney that Ripley made the first broadcast ever done from Australia to New York. A host of technical problems beset the endeavor but, with the *Mariposa* waiting to proceed, Rip finally shouted a greeting into the microphone, autographed the mike for the Aussie technicians, and sprinted back onto the ship.

Ripley and Friml became constant companions on the trip. They shared an interest in Eurasian women and in the Orient. Rip was properly appreciative of the Lucullan delights that Friml contrived. And as the leading celebrities aboard, they were called upon to do a shipwide broadcast from the lounge. With a host of Broadway credits to his name—"The Vagabond

King" and various "Ziegfeld Follies"—Friml took over during rehearsals and insisted on changing the dialogue. When the big night finally arrived he stunned Rip by wandering into the lounge, facing the mike first, then Rip, and asking, "Well, what am I supposed to say?" Rip's ad lib recovery is lost to history, but he managed to keep the show going. Thus, with this event, and the Sydney–New York broadcast, he was learning just enough about broadcasting to have mike fright when he eventually got around to his vastly successful career in radio.

That 1932 trip took Rip all over the Pacific and the Orient. He visited New Zealand, New Guinea, Hawaii, the Philippines, Bali, Celebes, Java, Malaya, Siam, Indochina, Hong Kong, Macao, Japan, and China. He was especially delighted by his trips to the smaller islands, where freedom and naturalness still was the dominant feature of native life—at Pago Pago in American Samoa and at Suva in the Fijis, among others. For his trip through the Dutch East Indies he had to transfer to a little Dutch boat, the *Melchoir Treub,* which plied between Bali, the Celebes, Java, and Sumatra.

Throughout this trip there was blazing color and fantastic detail for the artist's eye. Rip was struck by sizzling, polyglot Singapore, the magnificent Inner City (the Intramuros) of Manila, with its massive, beautiful seventeenth-century architecture. He was not prepared for what he saw when he arrived in Shanghai in the late spring of 1932, several weeks after the Japanese had moved in. Rip was taken to Chapei, a part of Greater Shanghai, and for the first time saw the fresh ravages of war; the still smoldering rubble, the constant burials, big bomb pits filled with foul green water, the lime piled up for the dead. Rip was stunned by the damage and the tales of what had happened: twelve thousand civilians killed and about a quarter of a million forced to seek refuge in the International Settlement, there to sleep in the streets or find shelter in warehouses and churches.

In the midst of the devastation, Shanghai's famed night life was going full blast, and Rip found that much to his liking. He went to the St. George, a sailor's saloon and dance hall, and then to Del Monte's, Shanghai's after-hours hot spot outside the city where revelers always wound up in the morning. Ripley had heard that among the pleasures to be sampled in Shanghai were the "Del Monte Girls," so that when the evening was over, one of them accompanied him back to the Cathay Hotel—a place he appropriately renamed "The Cat Hotel."

Ripley went on to Peking, to Manchuria and then Japan before starting home. There were two sobering incidents en route. First, in order to get some variety in his travel, Rip transferred from the *Mariposa* to the *President Wilson*. Only after he had boarded the latter vessel did he discover that the esteemed Mr. Dollar, head of the Dollar Lines, had exercised a Prohibition Era option of keeping the ship dry. The second incident occurred after Rip had reached the United States. He decided to visit his birthplace, and when the word got out in Santa Rosa the mayor of that town invited him to city hall and there formally presented him with the ridgepole of the house in which Rip had been born. Ripley was touched to the point of tears by the affair and later used the pole in his fabulous island home, Bion.

In 1933 Ripley covered South America extensively. His "Believe It or Not" feature was very popular there, appearing in newspapers from Mexico City to Argentina. Moreover, the trips to that part of the world provided Ripley with an enormous amount of lively material. There were revolutionary heroes, brave Indians, ancient empires, insane emperors, mislaid mines that rivaled Solomon's. And always new women.

From a personal standpoint, Ripley also liked the "Old World Spanish" feeling about the cities. Rip never did make friends with the twentieth century.

There's no question that Ripley enjoyed remote places, such as the Orient, North Africa, and even South America as it was in the early 1930s, because he would not be held too rigidly accountable for the facts. In this sense Rip was a storyteller —entertaining, amusing, occasionally enthralling, but not particularly pretending to educate or instruct. He appeared to be genuinely amused when he was called "The World's Biggest Liar." For an introduction to one collection of his works he repeated an apt saying, "This world is all a fleeting show, for man's illusion given."

One of the comparatively few occasions on which Ripley sought the more serious attention of his readers was after a trip to Russia in 1934. He was a diehard conservative before he went there, and even more so after his return. In a speech made after his return he told of his experiences.

"A year ago I found myself on the border of Russia and Persia. The Persians had left me and my baggage exactly in the middle of the international bridge at Julfa where it crosses the Araxes River—the boundary line between Russia and Persia. I was completely abandoned—and totally isolated. The Red soldiers at the Russian end of the bridge wouldn't let me across, and the Persian soldiers at the other end wouldn't let me return. So there I sat in 'no man's land' for about five hours.

"Finally some Soviet officials aroused themselves long enough to put me through a microscopic examination. They turned my baggage inside out searching for arms and money, and pried into every piece of paper I had in search of anti-Communist propaganda. Then, after seizing my three cameras, I was permitted to set foot in Russia—the 'Communist paradise.'

"Believe It or Not—it is not a paradise but a paradox. Russia is a gigantic poorhouse where millions of people are on the verge of starvation at this moment. Outside of Moscow and Leningrad—the Soviet show places—starvation stalks through squalor and filth. Moscow and Leningrad are show places—and fake shows at that—where the traveler is led about under a smoke screen of propaganda and allowed to see only what they want him to see and nothing else. You are shown the Kremlin, Lenin's tomb, a 'model' farm, a 'model' workers' club, and various other 'models.'

"But there are no model conditions in the outlying rural districts of the Ukraine and the Caucasus. I had no food for the first two days after crossing the border from Persia. Ragged, starving mobs crowded to the train windows begging and crying for food."

Rip went on in that vein, and earned the undying enmity of U.S. communists. They kept up a drumfire of attacks in the Communist press; they picketed his public appearances; they ridiculed him. And Ripley appreciated every line of type and every rude gesture on the picket line. Among the homilies that Ripley would recite was the one that went: "Every knock is a boost."

Over the years Rip recorded impressions about many of the places he visited and a random selection of them indicates his thinking about a wide variety of things: "If I could be reincarnated, I'd return as a Chinese"; "The Samoans have escaped the worst curse of Christianity—they never wear shoes at any time."

For reasons which will be left to the psychologists, Ripley always equated Christianity with the wearing of clothes, especially shoes. This might simply have resulted from the fact that his feet always hurt. He once met a native king in Fiji who had, Ripley said, consumed some fifteen hundred humans in his cannibal existence. But now he was reformed and had become a Christian convert. How could Rip tell? "He was wearing knickers. As soon as they start wearing clothes, the church has them."

"In Turkey, all the men wear red fezes, which they never take off . . . and all the soldiers wear big swords which *they* never take off. More soldiers are stabbed trying to sit down in the coffee houses than ever were on a battlefield."

"Italian women are the best I've ever seen. They have the two best features a woman can have—good legs and fine eyes."

"Naples had the best art gallery in the world." This was a gallery of salacious art, and admission was by special permission only. Rip got permission.

"The most beautiful sight I've ever seen is the Glowworm Cavern of New Zealand . . . like a soundless paradise."

"Dinnertime in New Zealand is the most dismal hour of the day. They never speak a word during mealtime, just work away at their food."

"The greatest sight is right here in the United States—the Grand Canyon."

Although Ripley practiced no particular religion, religion per se attracted him. Observing that, "Strange is man when he seeks after his gods," Bob reached the conclusion that the strangest places on earth were the holiest. Continuing from this premise, he declared, "The strangest and most remarkable city in the world is the holy city of Benares on the muddy arm of the Ganges, India's holy river." Considering how widely traveled Ripley was, it was a remarkable statement.

The Indian ascetics continually held him enthralled. The physical tortures these men inflicted upon themselves were a constant marvel to Ripley. Many of his cartoons featured these fakirs, such as the man who hung head down for three hours at a time, or the man who had gazed into the sun for fifteen years. The firewalkers, the bed-of-nails men—these were all grist for the Ripley mill.

So intense was Ripley's admiration for the genuine article that he became enraged at those vaudeville performers who claimed to be able to go into cataleptic trances or put others into them.

"The various 'Rama Beys' etc. who have been appearing in American vaudeville recently with 'buried alive' acts in which they claim the power to suspend animation are merely tricksters," he wrote, with more heat than was his wont. "None of them ever saw India—as a matter of fact, the most successful one is an Italian. Houdini did the same trick under water."

Bob was almost childishly pleased with whatever honors accrued to him as a result of his travels. He took—understandably—great pride in adding the letters "F. R. G. S."—Fellow of the Royal Geographical Society—after his signature. This was heady stuff to the self-educated Ripley, as were the various honorary degrees he received—Master of Arts from Dartmouth, Doctor of Letters from Missouri Valley College, and a Doctorate of Oratory from Staley College.

In eventually making up his list of two hundred and one countries which he had visited, Ripley wasn't overly technical. He listed, for example, the Virgin Islands and also St. Thomas and St. Croix, which happen to be two of the Virgin Islands. Listed, too, are both Salvador and El Salvador. It probably would have disturbed his fellow fellows of the Geographical Society to note that he tabulated, as "countries" he visited, the Shetland and Orkney islands, Sark, the Isle of Man, Gibraltar, Hong Kong, Malta, Sicily, and Corsica.

If Ripley stretched a point or two in selecting both countries and capitals to tote up his complete score of two hundred and one nations he may be excused, since every new spot was a new country as far as Bob was concerned; and, more important, there were very few countries unvisited by Ripley. He had a genuine love of travel, a fondness and appreciation of faraway spots. If they weren't already historical, he felt that his arrival there compensated for that.

In reporting on his travels, Ripley made as much capital out of disappointments as he did from the startling, spectacular sights and sounds. After visiting the Garden of Eden, he said, "I was disappointed in the Garden of Eden. It's a desolate place, and there are no fig trees, and no apple trees either. Hell (Norway) is much more attractive. It's often been suggested that I go there. And I do."

This was the way he introduced the subject of Hell to his public. In private, he explained that he had pledged as a virile young man to make love in as many countries and strange places as possible—"even in Hell." During one European trip he made a long detour to visit Hell, and, with a girl picked up in a café, made good on his pledge. He also had a photo taken of himself with the mayor of that town, for use in publicity. For Rip, that was a pretty good mixture of business and pleasure.

CHAPTER VII

Ripley, on Land

ALL that was most admirable and most shocking in the life of Bob Ripley—as well as all that was most startling and spectacular—came to the fore at Bion, the fabulous island estate at Mamaroneck, New York, which he bought in 1934. The only staid and unimaginative thing about Bion was its name, taken from the initials of "Believe It or Not."

Here he lavishly entertained the famous and mighty—great sports figures like Jack Dempsey and Babe Ruth; national heroes; and stars of stage, screen, and radio—as well as the little-known, including aides on his newspaper and radio projects. Here he displayed a moving devotion to dumb animals, and a hair-raising callousness to some human beings. And here he maintained a fantastic collection of objects and *objets d'art* gathered in his restless travels around the world.

There's no question that Bion was Rip's proudest possession. He could have owned homes before this, but he preferred to stay at the New York Athletic Club until he found just the right place to match his mood and aspirations—or, natively shrewd businessman that he was, perhaps he was waiting until he could get just the right bargain on just the right place.

The previous owner of Bion was John Eberson, an internationally known theatrical architect. The property, including a house built at the turn of the century, was practically derelict when Eberson took it over. He spent many thousands of dollars improving the place—installing mosaic columns from the Middle East, exquisite wood paneling bought at auction from a Park Avenue mansion, and other items from the Armour home in Chicago. But Eberson was unable to maintain this luxury, and Ripley picked it up for $85,000. Rip never toted up how much he put into redecorating and furnishing the place, but certainly it represented hundreds of thousands of dollars before he was done with it.

Ripley loved everything about Bion, including the approach to it, along a winding road called Taylor's Lane, which branched off the Boston Post Road, twisting for a mile or so until it reached a causeway that linked the mainland with Rip's island. Taylor's Lane is locally famed as the oldest road in Mamaroneck, a town which dates back at least three centuries. This sort of thing pleased Ripley mightily, the oldest, smallest, biggest, and other variations on the superlative being his stock in trade.

The sight that met a guest as he crossed the one-lane causeway was of an enormous and imposing house of twenty-nine rooms, set upon an island of about three acres in the middle of a small cove. The house was constructed of stucco painted a light cream, with dark brown wood trim, and stone. It was of a type known in the United States as English Tudor, and in England as "stockbroker Tudor," a telltale sign of the *nouveau riche*. Some of the leaded casement windows were of stained glass. A wide stone porch ran along the back of the main floor, and some of the upper rooms had small balconies with iron railings, in the fashion of old New Orleans.

From the causeway to the entrance was a short driveway. The entrance was on a small turnabout which circled a huge oak tree. There Rip would often meet guests, to take them on a foot tour of the island before subjecting them to his boundless hospitality indoors.

Ripley's house stood foursquare on a mount of solid rock, which was the highest point in the island, about fifteen feet above the water. Undoubtedly this site was selected by the original builder because of the savage storms which often swept along Long Island Sound from the Atlantic, bringing a quick rise in the tidal level. A strong sea wall ran completely around the island, although even that did not prevent Bion from going under water on occasion; but the house itself was never damaged.

In the terrible hurricane which lashed Long Island Sound on September 21, 1938, the island went under water, sea wall and all. Rip's place, like those around him, was badly buffeted, but he and his guests managed to ride out the storm. Situated as it was on the high mound of rock, Ripley's house remained fairly dry.

Not only did the house on Bion stand off the hurricane, but through some strange freak it managed to maintain its electric power. Douglas Storer, Rip's manager, alarmed over the safety of his client and friend, sped to Bion after the storm had spent itself and the roads once again were passable. What Storer saw was a weird sight—there was the house at night, rising above the black waters like a volcanic peak from the ocean floor, and fully lighted, a huge beacon in the surrounding darkness.

Although the little body of water surrounding Bion was called Van Arminge Pond, after its owner of a century earlier, it was not a pond at all, but a cove, or inlet, of Long Island Sound. The relation of the island to the cove would be, roughly, like that of a golf ball enclosed by a horseshoe. The original owners took advantage of this natural formation and built a gristmill at the mouth of the cove, where it entered the sound. One of the obligations of owning the house on Bion was that the owner must maintain, at his own expense, the dam at the mouth of the cove. Owners of other properties around the cove were free to enjoy the pond, plus the right "to clam and other shelling."

The pond was good for small boats, and Ripley had a navy all his own on it. It was the strangest fleet ever assembled by any one man, with boats of all shapes and sizes, running from an Alaskan kayak to a Seminole dugout. Bob also had a gufa boat from the East, made of woven reeds in the shape of a huge round basket and waterproofed with pitch. It was practically unsinkable, but only a skilled oarsman could do anything with it except make it go in circles. In the Ripley navy also were sidewheel paddleboats, canoes, and plain old rowboats.

Ripley just about broke even between the pleasure the pond brought him in showing off his weird navy to visitors and the trouble it caused him. It was not good for swimming, as it was filled with vegetation and had a soft bottom. Its stagnancy in the summer months not only made it malodorous but also a great breeding spot for mosquitoes. Summer evenings on the island were unpleasant until the advent of DDT when Rip had widespread, regular spraying done.

For swimming, Bob had a regular beach on the sound, near the southern arm of the cove, complete with a small rocky shore and a good dock, with water deep enough for his junk and a large power boat. The beach, because of the stones, was not comfortable to the feet of Ripley or any of his guests, but it was a problem he never was able to overcome. No matter how many tons of sand he brought in to cover the stones, it all was washed away by the following season, because of the current at the mouth of the cove. Bob, an obstinate man, for years kept trying for a sandy beach, without success. He consoled himself by admiring the shore in front of movie magnate Spyros Skouras's home, on the opposite side of the cove.

"Look at that lovely beach," Ripley would direct visitors. "It was all formed with my sand washed over there from here."

One of the prettiest sights on Bion was the long narrow footbridge which led from the island to the dock and beach, crossing the cove from the point at which the boathouse stood. It was delicate and slender in its construction, gaily painted in white, yellow, blue, and scarlet. Viewed on a sunny summer's day, against the background of the towering green trees, its bright colors and delicate outline reflected in the dark, still waters, it was a scene no visitor ever forgot.

One of the many contradictory sides of Ripley's personality was his love of animals. If you went out of your way a little, going from the house to the boathouse or the beach, you would come across a quiet little spot hidden among the trees and shrubs. No more than twelve feet square, it was marked by low, round cement posts, embedded with small, colored stones. This was Rip's dog cemetery, where many of his pets were buried, and those of many of his friends.

Ripley had a genuine fondness for animals. It was only to his pets that he ever gave true gentleness and sustained affection. It wasn't maudlin, but a strong attachment and sense of responsibility. Walking the grounds at Bion, Ripley always carried a pocketful of nuts to hand-feed the squirrels and chipmunks with which the island abounded.

Ripley's dislike of anything resembling cruelty to animals frequently resulted in visitors' becoming the victims of violent tirades if they made any boasts of their hunting prowess. Rip had nothing but contempt for all hunters, including the big-game hunters who made safaris to Africa.

"Shooting a lion in the wilds of Africa is no different from taking a gun and killing the family cow in a man's back yard!" Ripley once shouted at an astonished guest. "You're no better than a murderer!"

Ripley kept many dogs on the island, including two beautiful coal-black spaniels, Virtue and Sin, registered as Ripley's Virtue and Barnacle Bill, and descended from the greatest spaniel of all time, My Own Brucie. Bob never showed these dogs but bred some very fine dogs from them, including the pet he was fondest of, the prizewinner, Cinder. He also had collies, Dalmatians, and sheepdogs.

Along with these common breeds of animal, Ripley maintained some less conventional specimens. On his first weekend visit to Bion, Joe Connolly was startled during an early-morning walk to come face-to-fangs with a twenty-eight-foot boa constrictor. Joe retreated posthaste to his room and wouldn't leave the house for the rest of the weekend.

"Don't worry, Joe, he's a friend of mine," Rip kept telling him with uncontrolled glee. He explained—but not to Connolly's satisfaction—that the boa, named Gertie, was kept placid on a steady diet of rabbits.

Bugs Baer was another friend of Ripley who was discouraged from visits to Bion by Gertie's presence. One day Rip called his dear friend and invited him out, telling him that he had made a novel pen for the reptile, a circle of broken glass.

"Y'know, Bugs, a snake won't cross broken glass," Rip promised.

"Let me tell you something," Bugs replied. "Neither will I."

Rip thereafter shipped Gertie off to a zoo.

The navy and pets of Ripley were only part of the outdoor attractions at Bion. All over the island he placed items from his fantastic collection which were too large to go in his house

—totem poles he had brought back from Alaska; a giant shell of a man-eating clam; an ancient bronze soldier on horseback; a huge Alaskan warrior fully rigged out for battle; a stone grouping of the three Chinese monkeys who saw no evil, heard no evil, and spoke no evil; a small, naked bronze boy making the usual fountain, to the embarrassment of shy visitors. The grounds of the island were well kept, and contained many beautiful trees and rare shrubs and plants which Ripley had collected in the course of his globe-trotting.

As you entered the grounds, there was a sight which should have sent many of Ripley's visitors running screaming to the nearest lodge of Alcoholics Anonymous, considering the habits of the vast majority of his guests. The entrance to the tiny causeway was guarded by two huge bronze Chinese figures, with bulging bellies, ferocious faces, and arms uplifted in threatening gestures. Mounted on stone pedestals, those bronze figures, each of which weighed literally a ton, formed a unique portal.

"They are Chinese," explained Rip to more than one guest. "They're supposed to ward off evil spirits."

The entrance to the house was comparatively simple, considering the general layout. It was just a flight of divided stone steps, leading to a very wide wood-paneled entrance hall, which ran the length of the house, all the way to the back door, which gave onto the stone porch. There Rip set up tables for his more elaborate buffet luncheons on warm days.

Ripley probably was the only man in the world whose taste in interior decorating began with his feet. For a man who was a better-than-average athlete well into his thirties, Rip had what is known to the sports world as "bum dogs." His feet always hurt him, and in later years would become painfully swollen. One of the highest honors Rip could bestow on the more favored of his female guests was to allow them the privilege of massaging his feet.

Because of his foot trouble, Ripley went in, in a big way, for a profusion of soft, expensive Oriental rugs, purchased from Persia and China, India and Turkey. Most of his guests believed Rip had selected them for their richness and coloring, but actually it was because he walked around so often in his bare feet.

Inside the center hall, which was dimly lighted by a single stained-glass window over the stairs, was a homemaker's nightmare. Ripley had a simple rule of thumb in assembling his furniture—it had to be expensive and heavy. He confused tonnage with taste, and his idea of interior decorating could best be described as "mixed-up international." The furniture was Spanish and Italian and had an over-all Gothic look to it. There was a long refectory table down the center, flanked by a series of chairs straight out of the Renaissance—high, straight-backed, hard, uncompromising, and thoroughly uninviting.

A huge stone fireplace, spacious enough to roast an ox in, had the idea ever occurred to Bob, took up a good part of one side of this center hall. The walls were hung with more ornaments of stone, iron, and brass than decorated any ducal palace since the days of Lorenzo the Magnificent. The fact that most of the decorations were weapons—spears, masks, crossbows, and pieces of armor—gave it a medieval appearance. An incongruous note—and there were many to be found in any of Ripley's residences—was a large translucent lamp which was made from the belly of a camel and which always glowed in the center of the long table.

Ripley had—but obviously not on display for all his guests —a truly amazing collection of erotica, ranging from the revolting to the exquisitely executed. These, of course, were shown only to the discerning, and had to be carefully handled. It also pleased this morbid genius to have a large collection of pictures of freaks and of deformities caused by leprosy and elephantiasis. While Rip's erotic collection frequently raised eyebrows, the latter collection could raise the latest meal of the squeamish visitor.

If Ripley detected a note of queasiness among his guests, he was likely to document the pictures with recitals of first-hand experience. "I'll never forget," he would begin, "the first case of elephantiasis I ever saw. I was walking along a road in Shanghai and thought I saw a beggarman sitting against a wall holding a huge brass bowl. When I got closer I saw that it was the man's stomach! His lower belly was so swollen that the skin, drawn taut, actually glistened in the sun. It also appeared to have been oiled, to keep it from cracking.

"Horrible sight," Rip would conclude with gusto, doing everything but smacking his lips. "The disease is transmitted by a mosquito, you know."

The last clinical observation assumedly boomed the sale of mosquito netting all along the Atlantic Seaboard.

On the same floor as the living room was a small suite of bedrooms which were in a little wing of their own. These must have been quite a comfort and solace to Ripley's overnight guests who were recoiling from the garishness of the displays in the living room, for they were furnished in a homey, small-town Grand Rapids style.

You entered the hall to these rooms by way of a very plain and well-worn wooden door. This had been made by Bob's carpenter father for the house he had built in Santa Rosa, the house in which Ripley had been born. Rip was most sentimental about this door, and it still bore the metal numerals of his Santa Rosa street address.

Ripley's theory—"If it's big, it has to be good"—was nowhere more fully demonstrated than in the huge guest bath on the first floor in his Mamaroneck home. This room, used by women guests for changing, had a Scotch spray shower, soft rugs, and a wall of sliding mirrors, behind which was a long closet filled with every necessity for swimming, sunbathing, or merely getting clean after an afternoon's romping on the grounds. Slippers, bathing suits, and caps and robes were there in all sizes and shapes. It was well stocked with mounds of clean, fluffy towels, mats, fragrant soaps, talcums and oils, bobby pins and sun lotion. You name it and Bob had it. It had the general appearance of an Elizabeth Arden annex. Some of Ripley's guests—indeed, most of them—might have found him an unusual host, but none found him an inconsiderate one.

Although Ripley loved every room in the house, he was more at home in his large, airy studio on the top floor than anywhere else. Here, perhaps, he was happiest of all, for this was where he and his art assistants worked.

High up over the sound, with a splendid panoramic view of its lovely shores, his drawing board resting against the desk, Ripley was in his element. His sure hand working quickly and confidently, expressing with black ink on white Ross board exactly what he wanted to, Rip, for all his traveling, was in the world he knew best.

A happy and contented man, he worked facilely and quickly, pausing now and then to dip into the little wooden box of cracked corn which he kept on his window sill, to feed the little creatures who were his daily visitors—chipmunks and squirrels and brightly colored little birds, as well as the bold and venturesome common sparrow. It was this Ripley his friends like to recall best, the Ripley who was in the house he loved, doing the work he loved, and surrounded by the little wild creatures he loved.

There were some large bedrooms and baths on this top floor, in addition to Rip's studio. One of these rooms the artist reserved for special guests. And a special guest in Ripley's home didn't necessarily mean somebody in the VIP tradition of today, a person of prominence who could further the host socially or businesswise. A special guest in the Ripley home was simply someone Bob was fond of, someone, perhaps, who had befriended him long ago, someone whose company he enjoyed.

This room was done completely in Chinese style. The walls were decorated with Chinese prints and silk hangings. All the furniture, which consisted of a double bed, a dressing table, night table, chest of drawers, and assorted chairs, was made of a heavy wood enameled with a lacquer of vivid gold and scarlet. Each piece was profusely decorated with dragons in high relief and intricately carved birds and flowers. The dragons, protruding about a foot from the flat surfaces, swarmed all over the furniture, crawling among the flowers and birds. It was an overpowering room, and one in which no Chinese would be found dead, but it made a great hit with the Occidentals.

Despite the bizarre decoration there is little doubt that the guests found the room restful—once they closed their eyes. The mattress was the finest product of Western civilization, a no-nonsense innerspring affair.

On the restful bed was a handsome, beautifully worked silk coverlet. This was the handiwork of Rip's housekeeper, Mrs. Doud, a skilled needleworker and a woman of excellent taste. It was she who taught Ripley a great deal about the fine work of fabrics and the art that goes into their making. The coverlet was partly Chinese embroidery into which she had carefully blended her own work.

Ripley's own bedroom was down the hall from his studio

and the guest room. It was, in contrast to the other rooms, practically a cloistered cell—not that it was monastic. Lacking many of the gimcracks and gewgaws which dominated other rooms in the house, it appeared to be sparsely furnished.

Bob couldn't resist one gimmick in his bedroom, however. It had one highly unusual piece of furniture, an eighteenth-century Spanish vargueno, or traveling desk, which he claimed was a poison cabinet of the Borgias. He told the gullible it had a secret spring and that anyone who tried to open it would be injected with a fatal poison. Everybody took his word for it.

The other furniture also was dark and heavy, with Spanish-Italian overtones. Rip slept in a three-hundred-year-old Italian walnut canopy bed. The bed was large, a hand-carved affair, as were the few chairs and tables in the room also. There were a couple of modest, and expensive, prints on the wall, but the dominating feature of the décor was a huge painting, seven feet across, of a life-sized female nude engaged in what seemed to be a two-falls-out-of-three wrestling match with a cobra. From the painting, executed by an artist named Ferrier, it was difficult to determine which was winning.

"I never knew," said one visitor to another, "that Bob's fondness for wrestling would lead him to purchase a painting like this. Sensational, isn't it?"

"Either sensational or sensual," said the second guest.

Perhaps one of the strangest features of the home on Bion —and you put your neck out when you single out one over another—was a fully equipped steam room and gymnasium. This was no doubt a result of Bob's long stay at the New York Athletic Club. Ripley was a firm believer in the recuperative powers of a thorough steaming-out for those who had over-indulged the previous night. Bob was equally convinced that physical exercise was a greater means to health than Florence Nightingale and the Mayo brothers combined.

Because his Mamaroneck home was set on rock, it had no true cellar. The small area which did go underground was given over almost completely to the steam room and gymnasium. Ripley used it almost daily, and always invited his guests to share its therapeutic benefits with him.

As any description of any home of Ripley's leads to tales of Bob's hospitality, it is obvious that the bar in the home on Bion rates special mention. Opening off the right side of the main hall, the bar was the focal point for parties large or small. You stepped down into it from a small doorway and found yourself in a cool, pleasantly dark, but not dungeon-like, room, low-ceilinged, with paneled wood on one side and carved-out rock on the other (it had been a wine cellar, under earlier owners). At the far side was the bar itself, not particularly large, but fully equipped.

Rip was proud of the bar, as well he should be. He delighted in "getting behind the stick" and serving. Bob would mix drinks enthusiastically, although with something less than a chemist's eye for the exactness of proportions. His own libation gave him no trouble. It usually was a slug of gin, to which he added water or grapefruit juice from time to time.

The room was pleasantly relaxing, like an old-fashioned tavern. There were some benches and an old leather chair, possibly the only article of furniture in the entire house that was old without having a story behind it. Somebody said Ripley took it from the lobby of the New York Athletic Club on a dull night. Set into the rock on the far side was a skeleton of an old wine cask, which went from floor to ceiling.

Ripley had the low ceiling of the bar so loaded with curios and with what he thought were pieces of art that a first-time visitor imagined himself in a storeroom of a museum which was on the edge of bankruptcy. There were odd bull whips, made from part of the bull's anatomy, and also a whale whip, which was called by the Eskimos *tokazrookowuzrokearpigigpokiviornarpok.*

"It may sound funny and it may look funny," Rip would say in explaining this odd ornamentation, "but it was very dear to the whale."

There was a circular lamp made of small beer kegs in the center of the room. The lamp was flanked by all sorts of odd bells, strung on either leather or rods. There were sheep bells, llama bells, reindeer bells and camel bells. It probably upset Rip that he didn't have the bells from Prancer, Dancer, Donner, Blitzen, and the rest of Santa Claus's original team.

Ripley permitted himself one sentimental gesture in the bar, the aforementioned ridgepole of the house in which he had been born in Santa Rosa.

From an aesthetic and economic point of view, the high point of Ripley's barroom decorations was his collection of steins and tankards. These must have been among the world's finest, assuming there were others so eccentric as to make such a collection. They were everywhere in the bar, and came from everywhere in the world—China, Germany, Italy, Norway—from Alaska to Africa. They ranged in size from less than an inch in height to four feet and were made of every known material. There were some richly ornamented goblets, called *pokals,* as well as containers made of pewter, wood, sterling silver, copper, bronze, gold, iron, ivory, leather, bone—to say nothing of the most delicately glazed porcelain, fragile as an eggshell. They were made of anything that was not porous.

Many of them were quite old, some going back to the sixteenth century, and had been gathered from all over the world, not omitting Colonial America. Some were truly works of art, intricately carved, filigreed, and jeweled.

Some were reputed to have a historical significance, such as the Russian "Cup of Sorrow." This was a memorial cup which Czar Nicholas II decided to give to his peasants and serfs as a souvenir of his coronation. It really was a rather unpretentious china mug, having no handles, but Ripley was vehement in defending its authenticity. He maintained that it was one of the gifts causing a stampede which killed five thousand people in a field near Moscow at the coronation ceremonies on May 30, 1896.

In the wine cask on the far side of the Ripley rathskeller from the bar were two low portals cut out of stone. These led to a series of little grotto-like rooms, unfurnished but not undecorated, since Ripley had far more ornaments than he had rooms, even in this spacious house. The caves on the left side of the cask served as a passageway that led to the lawn side of the house; while those on the other side were padlocked—housing, as they did, some items in Ripley's collection which he didn't care to exhibit to most of his guests.

The house sprawled over four levels, and many of Bob's visitors did the same. Each floor was laid out differently, which gave the house great variety and brought to the visitor the element of surprise, assuming the visitor was any longer capable of being surprised.

From the baronial entrance hall a broad, polished open stairway, the walls of which were hung with fine tapestries and rugs, zigzagged at right angles to a broad landing. On this landing was a tiny room like a booth, complete with chair, stand, and telephone in which a guest might privately receive or send a call.

The landing also led directly to the main living room, a long, lofty room with spacious windows facing out toward the

sound on one side and the Westchester mainland on the
other. The view, particularly on the sound side, was beautiful,
and it would have been a bird watcher's delight, for there was
an island sanctuary not far from Bion, and this entire area
was one of the great flyways between Canada and the South.

From the far end of this spacious living room, french doors
led to a round terrace, parapeted to give a battlement effect.
Narrow steps curved from the terrace to the lawn below. On
this terrace Rip had one of his proudest possessions, a giant
compass. Embedded in the polished stone of the terrace was
a narrow hoop of brass, forming a circle about ten feet in
diameter. From the center of the circle to the rim were narrow
brass strips, like spokes in a wheel. Each pointed in the exact
direction of one of the world's capitals. The name of the city,
and the exact distance in air miles, was lettered in brass. It
was a quaint conceit of Ripley to have the air-mile distance,
not from New York to the foreign city, but from Bion.

It is doubtful whether any other private home, no matter
how sumptuous, had such a decoration. When the New York
Daily News moved into its new building on East Forty-second
Street, Publisher Joseph Medill Patterson—like Ripley, a rug-
ged individualist—had a compass somewhat similar to this set
in the floor of the lobby.

Ripley furnished this living room in the gaudy manner in
which the homes of the wealthy were decorated in that period before the midget sat in the lap of J. Pierpont Morgan.
The style, according to one visitor, was "pre-Wall Street
crash, pre-FDR." In short, the room looked as Cain's ware-
house must have looked when *Life With Father* finally completed its record-breaking run on Broadway.

Yet a discerning visitor might find in this ornate conglom-
eration truly fine pieces of art. In beautiful cabinets of glass
and wood, Ripley had some of the best pieces of his amazing

collection—delicate porcelains, tiny illuminated books, valuable carvings in ivory and quartz.

One of the features of the room—indeed, as far as Bob was concerned, it was *the* feature—was the fireplace, handsomely carved and imposing. Over the long mantel was a mirror, which looked like any other reflecting glass until Ripley snapped on a light switch. Then the mirror became a window, and behind it was the framed original "Believe It or Not" cartoon which he had submitted to Walter St. Denis of the old *Globe* in 1918. It is a measure of Ripley's pride in himself that he believed this to be worthy of its special setting. When a guest questioned the propriety of the cartoon's being exhibited among so many genuine masterpieces, Bob snorted and said, "If it weren't for that, these wouldn't be here." The cartoon was the original and not a reproduction, and included Ripley's first thought for a caption, "Champs and Chumps," which had been penciled out and "Believe It or Not" substituted.

For the large parties outdoors in summer, Ripley had installed a fine wiring system for lights and loud-speakers. Some of these parties, particularly those inspired for business or publicity reasons, ran to nearly a hundred guests. Rip's talent for showmanship was evident here, for there was no scrimping or stinting, and the cookouts were elaborate affairs, with as many as six chefs working over the fires. The steaming cauldrons of clams, lobsters, and ears of corn, the beds of gleaming hot coals for the steaks, made an unforgettable sight. Those invited talked about it for days, which didn't harm Ripley's position with his radio sponsors.

The parties were day-long affairs, with announcements continually blaring over the loud-speakers of swimming and boating contests that were about to start or of lineups that were being chosen for the softball game. Rip enjoyed the ball

game, invariably organized it, and played in it until he became somewhat enfeebled. Even then, he frequently insisted
upon umpiring.

It was natural that many of Ripley's house guests were famous in their own line, but there were many he invited who
had no particular talent or reputation. His guests were as
variegated as the outlandish décor of his homes. Many believed that Bob bolstered his innate shyness by surrounding
himself with people dependent upon his bounty. Playing lord
of the manor seemed to make Ripley supremely happy, even
though he sometimes went quietly off to bed at the height of
the festivities.

Some friends thought Rip assuaged the memory pangs of
his early struggles through his bountifulness, but probably he
simply liked having people around him, provided he did the
selecting. While it soothes the peculiar egos of some to play
host to "name" guests, it is a matter of record that many who
accepted Bob's hospitality were unknown when they were invited and just as anonymous when they left.

Few people had greater pride in their possessions than Ripley. He enjoyed conducting guided tours around his home,
making the disclosure of the original "Believe It or Not" cartoon the *pièce de résistance* of the tour. Off his huge living
room was a small adjoining room, probably the only uncluttered spot on the premises. In this room, dimly lighted
by a few tall cathedral-like casement windows at one end,
was a velvet-covered table on which reposed Ripley's collection of paste replicas of European crowns, orbs, scepters, and
royal tiaras. Also on this table were replicas of all the famous
diamonds in the world, the Hope, Jonker, Cullinan, Koh-i-
noor, Polar Star, and other gems which had achieved international prominence.

The room had a domed ceiling, painted blue and studded

with gilt stars. At the far end of the room was an enormous
painting, a canvas which reached almost from ceiling to floor
and extended from wall to wall. The painting, executed in
about 1880 by the Russian, C. Makoffsky, was called "The
Choosing of the Bride." It depicted the ceremony of a young
girl becoming the wife of a Russian nobleman and receiving
the blessing of the Church.

The canvas was crowded with figures, not only of the bridal
pair, but of the families of each. Nearly twenty figures were
in the scene, and were startlingly lifelike, for Makoffsky was
an artist almost photographic in his execution of detail. When
Ripley brought his guests into this room suddenly, and without any intimation of what they were to see, the effect was
startling. You felt as if you were seeing a living tableau.

Ripley, with the true artistic touch, had the floor of the
room covered in black and white tiles, precisely as the floor
was in the painting. Since the canvas reached the floor, the
tiles blended into each other, and you felt as though you were
actually in the room with the wedding group.

Makoffsky, while scarcely the Leonardo da Vinci of his day,
achieved a certain popularity in his lifetime. His "Choosing
of the Bride" was so highly thought of by Czar Nicholas II
that the latter did not want the picture taken from Russia.
Makoffsky, however, exhibited it at Antwerp in 1885, where
it received the Medal of Honor. When the picture went on
public sale, Nicholas II was one of the bidders but lost out
to a New York collector, Adolf Shuman, who is said to have
bid $60,000 for it. Ripley purchased it from the Shuman
estate.

There never was any full-scale cataloguing of Ripley's collection, although several starts were made. Quite probably
this was because there was so little system to the collection
itself. The commonplace and the banal ranked side by side

with what were truly collectors' items—behind the bar, with
its collection of steins, was a wooden chain of 365 identical
links, all carved from a single ten-foot piece of wood. Next to
the Iron Maiden of Nuremberg and authentic chastity belts
dating back to the Crusades was the amazing lifelike and life-
sized statue of a Japanese man, made by himself, an item
which Ripley also displayed in his New York apartment and
in his "Odditoriums."

In the midst of valuable works of art at Bion was a scale
model of the Eiffel Tower made from thirty thousand match-
sticks. It intrigued Rip, and he admired it equally as much
as the authentic pieces.

As varied as Bob's collection of objects artistic and otherwise was his assortment of house guests. They came in all
sizes, shapes, and sexes. They might stay for hours, days,
weeks, or months.

On one occasion a beautiful blond actress who was his
house guest briefly threw the female members of the entourage into a tizzy by (a) making time with Bob, and (b) fail-
ing to wash, except semi-occasionally. By her untidy habits
she managed to stop up the Bion plumbing totally—no mean
feat. When she left, Ripley simply referred to her as "the
dirtiest female I have ever known."

It could have been, of course, that the show-stopper and
plumbing-stopper had been the victim of a conspiracy on the
part of the entrenched members of the "harem." While they
never dared openly to challenge any of Bob's new attach-
ments, they were an ingenious lot and had ways of their own
of getting rid of any genuine threat by a Janey-come-lately.

One of Ripley's visitors at Bion was a singer who decided
to attract the attention of the lord and master by suicide attempts. She burst into the room, proclaiming that she had just
swallowed a bottle of aspirin, threw herself from the upper

balcony (a short drop), and brandished a knife, pointing it at her tilted, and tinted, bosom. All was done with a fine sense of timing and before an audience, which soon became callous to her threats of self-destruction. Despite Ripley's fondness for exotic female companions, the singer was never asked back. She opened and closed in one.

"That goofy broad loused up the whole weekend," explained Rip.

The French have amorous phrases both apt and fascinating, but Ripley ran them off the boards. After he was established at Bion he sometimes had as many as four or five female house guests in residence. It could have been that Rip believed there was safety in numbers. Skillfully he played off one against the other, with the result that none of the girls was quite sure who was the current court favorite, including the favorite herself.

While the very plurality of his entourage insured Ripley against being engulfed in the seas of matrimony, it also made for considerable to-dos in his private and professional life. His lady friends were constantly jockeying for position to gain the inside rail. And Rip kept them guessing, from start to finish.

The intense desire of the gals to achieve the number-one position in Ripley's private Nielsen ratings had one unusual effect. Each of them was afraid to let (a) Rip or (b) any of the others out of her sight. The result made for some long nights, well before television had come up with the late-late show.

The efforts of the Ripley entourage to curry favor with the master caused complications on the road as well as at home. If Bob were scheduled to show up at a studio for a rehearsal, one of the women might casually remark, "I think I'll go to town and do a bit of shopping." This would be the signal for a mass exodus from Bion, and all four, five, or six would show up at the studio where Ripley was attempting to rehearse his radio show.

"*Les girls*" were not looked upon with favor by anybody connected with the Ripley radio program. To begin with, they usually arrived well fortified against a sudden freeze, their radiators carefully stocked with alcohol. They would descend upon the working people at the studio, giving liberal and unsolicited advice on subjects of which they were totally ignorant, even if they had been sober. The late Charlie Spear, the chief writer on the early Ripley shows, gave them the unflattering nickname of the "Broads' Brigade," and thereafter they were never known by any other name around the studios.

Strangely enough, the one person at the rehearsals who wasn't upset by the girls' appearance or their off-the-cuff suggestions was Ripley. He completely ignored them, although later, when they were reassembled at Bion, he might deliver a blast to one or all, for their attempts to court favor.

It seems probable that each of the girls thought, at one time or another, that Ripley might marry her. He never gave any even the merest hint of a promise to make a quick trip to the justice of peace, but each thought that, by making herself indispensable, she could grab the brass ring and the little band of gold. This was the reason Rip kept alternating them, like a Madison Avenue executive with five gray flannel suits. Singly, he might have fallen, but facing them en masse he resisted with a tenacity not seen since Custer at Little Bighorn.

There was a casualness in Ripley's relations with the ladies-in-waiting that served his ends. He thought nothing of inviting one and all to share a steam bath with him in his private sauna in the lower reaches of Bion.

Ed Dooley, a great quarterback at Dartmouth in the

twenties and later a Republican Congressman from West-chester County, remembers partaking in a softball game at Bion with several female Chinese guests. "It was a hot day, and several of the boys stripped to the waist to alleviate the heat," recalled Dooley. "I was a little surprised when the girls followed suit. It really made little difference, as you could not tell them apart."

Kenneth Webb, an agency representative of Ripley's news show, now retired and living in Los Angeles, recalls the rivalry among Rip's women friends.

"They vied with each other," related Webb, "to find *objets d'art* and unusual antiques for the famous collection he had amassed in his travels. They often accompanied him on his trips and were very jealous of that privilege. Once, going south on a trip to the West Indies, one of them, being Oriental, had been told she would not be permitted to land in a British colony. However, she came down to see him off at Penn Station in New York—and also to be sure that none of the other girls was going along. What she didn't know was that somebody else joined the party when the train reached Philadelphia."

The nonchalance with which Ripley played the female field is illustrated by an incident Mrs. B. A. Rolfe recalled. She and her band-leader husband entered a New York night club and found Rip seated there with a beautiful blonde. After the Rolfes were seated, Bob excused himself from his fair companion and went over to their table. "Do you know the name of the girl I'm with?" he asked them. They told Ripley they had never seen her before, and he was quite downcast. "I thought sure you'd know her name," he said. "I don't, and I'd certainly like to find out."

Ripley was a great one for throwing parties anytime, but particularly on Christmas, since he celebrated his birthday on that day. It pleased him to know that throughout most of the world people were having a good time on his birthday, although he was realist enough to concede that undoubtedly there were people celebrating that day who had never heard of him or of his "Believe It or Not" feature. It was not a pleasant thought, but there it was.

Most of the parties would have been considered eminently successful, but there was one that somehow didn't quite come off. There were only four guests at Bion that night. Rip had invited Bugs Baer, but the humorist had wisely declined, on the grounds that Christmas was a day which should be celebrated in the bosom of one's family. Although Ripley had arrayed himself in his brightest mandarin costume, complete with robe, hat, and brocaded slippers, he felt that something was lacking as he gazed around the yule table. It was a justifiable suspicion.

Ripley's guests were an old flame, her young son—an incredibly tall, gangling lad—and two actresses, one a French import, the other Chinese, and neither feeling any pain. The lad declined to sit at the not-so-festive board, because he had surfeited himself with malted milks prior to his arrival.

The old flame added little to the gaiety. As soon as she seated herself she took from her dress a framed photograph of her late husband, propped it up next to her plate, and periodically wept because he was no longer among the living. The actresses were far enough along to have reached the muttering stage. It seemed that each thought Bob had designs on the other, and both had designs on Bob. Meanwhile the bone of their contention stared morosely into space. With the widow still weeping, the dinner finally broke up when one of the actresses reached into the cadaver of the holiday turkey and drew out a fistful of stuffing. This she molded into a ball and flung in her rival's face.

Ripley looked on at this byplay with no noticeable enthusiasm, rose from the table, picked up the telephone, and called Baer's number.

"It's just as well you and Louise didn't come, Bugs," said Rip. "You probably wouldn't have had a very good time."

He was a man of endless facets, moods as unpredictable as catastrophe.

There was this Ripley:

A friend walked into the big house one afternoon and beheld there the potentate at joyfully relaxed leisure. Dressed in a Chinese gown, and stretched out on a chaise longue, he beamed like a friendly Oriental deity. And no wonder! Two of his handmaidens knelt at the foot of his couch, gently massaging his feet. He was at peace with all mankind.

But this could be Ripley, too.

My wife and I took a summer place just across Lake Bion from him in 1942, shortly after the birth of our son Barry. An almost daily visitor, particularly at times when Millie was nursing the baby, was one of the more entrancing flowers in Rip's harem. She was an exquisite creature of Chinese-Japanese mixture, given to the more colorful gowns of both cultures. She invariably paddled across the little body of water in a small boat, and made a delightful picture in a setting of quiet waters and great weeping willows that reached to the water's edge. Just as invariably, she always brought the baby a little flower, and would tuck it daintily behind his ear as he nursed. Then she would sit through the procedure, her lovely face sometimes fathoms deep in thought.

One Sunday, Rip invited us to one of his great parties. Millie, seeing the little Chinese-Japanese girl, sought her out and—in time—the two started a game of gin rummy. The first hand had hardly been dealt when Rip, in mikado's formal dress, loomed over them and barked to the girl, "How many times must I tell you not to mingle with my guests. Get off to your room!"

The girl ran, whimpering, out of the room. Millie went in search of her, to console her. She found her in a darkened little bedroom which featured decorations of cohabiting gods. The light fixture had been made from a Japanese parasol. The girl lay on the bed, sobbing.

In an effort to make her forget the ugliness of the scene below, Millie picked up a beautiful lacquered box from the dresser. "What exquisite work this is!" she said.

The girl took her face from her pillow and looked around. "Oh," she said; and then, after a bit: "I keep my baby's ashes in there."

Millie put it down swiftly, but sympathetically.

"Don't feel badly," the girl said. "They are not there now. When Bob gets mad at me he hides them."

Anyone who saw only this side of Ripley would have been properly repelled by the man. Many did, and were. Others who knew him—who could sympathize with the shyness he never overcame, who experienced his generosity, or wondered clinically what in the world bugged this enormously talented and lucky individual—were irresistibly drawn to him and on with him.

CHAPTER VIII

Ripley, the Broadcaster

THE radio industry in the 1930s drew many strange recruits from many strange places, but it is doubtful that any of these pioneers was stranger than Robert L. Ripley. And certainly never did so miscast a performer score so sweeping a success.

It was typical of the frenzy which marked those early days of radio that it should turn to an artist who performed with pen and ink for a medium which could capture only one sense, that of hearing. But radio sought desperately for something new, and preferably something that could not be easily imitated. That Ripley was a success on radio may seem incredible, after any rational examination of his performing talents, but his success is further proof of the magnetic attraction his "Believe It or Not" idea held for uncounted millions of people.

Rip made his first scheduled radio appearance in 1930, when he was interviewed on the "Collier Hour" by a fine editor of the era, John B. Kennedy. On that occasion he told the story of "The Marching Chinese." That stirred up enough interest to land him a series for Colonial Beacon Oil Company in April 1930, and shortly thereafter for Standard Oil. On these shows Rip just talked about his travels and recounted, as best he could, some of the weirder items from his voluminous "Believe It or Not" files. When these contracts expired there was no great rush of new sponsors in his direction.

A much more dramatic type of presentation was required than could be afforded by Rip's faltering delivery.

It was in 1933 that Ripley entered big-time broadcasting. Douglas F. Storer was producing the Hudson Motor Company show and, having heard Ripley in his early efforts, came up with the idea of dramatizing "Believe It or Not." The two men had never met, and the deal was arranged over transatlantic telephone, with Ripley in London. The first broadcast was in December 1933.

Radio was quite freewheeling in those days. There were no weeks of rehearsal to put a show on the air—just one rehearsal, and that usually a few hours before air time. Ripley showed up about an hour and a quarter before the show was to go on, and Storer's first glimpse of the headline and keystone of his show was startling. Bob was wearing a pale blue shirt, a batwing tie of flaming orange, a plaid jacket, fawn-colored slacks, and black-and-white sports shoes.

"You're Bob Ripley?" asked Storer, wanting to know the worst at once. When Ripley nodded in blushing acknowledgment, Doug handed him a script and tottered away, with the deep conviction that he was to have one of the shortest director-producer careers in radio history.

Ripley's duties on the show were minimal. All he had to do was read a thirty-second introduction to a dramatized "Believe It or Not" incident and at the end of the half-hour show authenticate the story and say good night.

It seemed simple. But Storer soon realized that even getting Ripley to nod would call for someone with the directorial talents of a David Belasco. Before the evening was over, he was a trembling wreck, and Ripley was even worse. The script shook in Ripley's hands. It fell to the floor, and in retrieving it, he almost succeeded in sending the microphone stand hurtling into the audience. He mumbled, stumbled, and sweated his way through his few lines. When the show ended, Ripley looked as though he had fought Floyd Patterson, and Storer felt as if he had.

After his muttered "Good night" Ripley reeled toward the control room, seeking a critical appraisal from Storer.

"H-h-how'd I d-do?" stammered Ripley.

"You need a little practice," answered Storer.

Somehow the public liked the show, and enough letters came in to cause the sponsors to invite Ripley back.

"Do you think he can come up with another original idea?" one of the advertising-agency men asked Storer.

"I don't see why not," replied Doug. "After all, he's been doing it daily for his syndicate for more than fifteen years."

The radio version of "Believe It or Not" thus was firmly launched, thanks to Storer, whose help Rip acknowledged in autographing a book for him: "To Douglas Storer—Who First Believed in *Believe It or Not*—With All The Best."

While Ripley's original broadcasts had consisted merely of reading a script into a microphone in a studio cubicle, Bob now found himself in the middle of a full-scale performance, complete with studio audience. There was a "name" orchestra conducted by the famous B. A. Rolfe, a male trio, the announcer, Curt Peterson, and a large cast for the dramatization of the story Ripley had selected from his library of "Believe It or Nots."

The scripts sound hilariously dated now, but they were rated the highest entertainment in the days when radio was forcing movie houses to give away dishes to keep their doors open. Ripley, for example, was introduced with tongue-twisting alliteration that seemed very funny at the time. Here are a few samples.

"And here is that tropical, timely tallyman of terrific, triple-tested, typhoonic, trustworthy, telegrammatical truthful tales . . ."

Another was: "And here is that canyon-crashing, creditable, captain-conquistador of continental, climax-capping cornucopias." Apparently after due consideration, "climax-capping cornucopias" was deleted and "concentrated classics" was penciled in. Whether this editing could be considered an improvement, deponent knoweth not.

Hudson Motors was introducing a new model, the long-since-extinct Terraplane, when Ripley joined the show as a regular on January 6, 1934, and, perforce, the band became "B. A. Rolfe and his Terraplane Orchestra." The announcer took due note of this with a zestful shout, "Okay, B.A.! Let's Terraplane into action with a song dedicated to the nation's recovery program: 'New Deal Rhythm.'"

Ripley was sandwiched into the program between such numbers as "New Deal Rhythm," "It's Only a Paper Moon," and a couple of visits to the Grand Central Palace, where announcers extolled all the new, new features of the new, new Terraplanes—"advanced draftless ventilation . . . finger-touch controls on a big eye-level instrument panel . . . dynamic streamlines . . . knee action . . . independent springing of the front wheels, called Axelflex"—an indication that commercials haven't changed or improved a great deal in a quarter of a century.

With the same format, Ripley started carrying the Standard Brands banner in 1935, switched his allegiance to General Foods in 1937 and to Royal Crown Cola in 1939. There was always plenty of sponsor cash. The show did have a very wide appeal, and the sponsor could count on some extra promotional value from the frequent major "scoops" which Rip aired, particularly exclusive interviews with people in the eye of the news and "demonstrations" of spectacular feats.

When Douglas Corrigan flew his light plane across the Atlantic to Dublin on July 17, 1938, the Ripley organization went into operation almost automatically. A few hours after Corrigan landed there was a telephone call from Storer. The result was one of Ripley's scoops. On the air, he held a two-way interview with "Wrong Way" in Dublin, the night after Corrigan's exploit. It was great timing; the entire country was enchanted with the nonchalant young pilot who, knowing he would never get clearance to fly the Atlantic, filed a flight plan for the West Coast. "A fellow can't help it if he gets mixed up, can he?" asked Corrigan on Ripley's program.

The same question might have been asked by Lou Gehrig, the Yankee first-base immortal, during his appearance on the program. Lou was involved in a classic mix-up. Ripley at the time was on the air for Huskies, a breakfast cereal competing with Wheaties. Each week a sports celebrity would come on for a brief interview, then do the commercial.

Ford Bond was the announcer and handled the interview. Then, with Gehrig, he came to the "plug." "Tell me, Lou," Bond asked, "what do you like most in the morning for breakfast?" Gehrig, his script at his side, beamed and responded, "I like nothing better than a big bowl of Wheaties!"

Bond was too astonished to attempt an ad-lib cover and just stood there gulping. Gehrig slapped the side of his head with his hand and walked to a neutral corner. Ripley watched from a distance, helplessly. There were about thirty seconds of stunned silence before the program continued on its way.

Even a boo-boo like this turned out for the best for Rip. News services carried stories of the slip-up to newspapers around the country, and the stories, of course, had to mention both Wheaties and Huskies. The sponsor, General Foods, was delighted.

One of Ripley's most unusual shows—and nearly all of them

were unusual—was the advent of Kuda Bux, the fire walker
from India. This may have been one of New York's greatest
free outdoor extravaganzas. It was in August 1938, and the
show was staged on a parking lot where the Radio City
garage now stands.

Ripley opened the program from inside the studio and then
went outside to do the blow-by-blow, or pitter-by-patter account of Kuda Bux walking through fire. Bob fairly drooled
as he related the treat in store for his listeners, to say nothing
of the thousands in the street who were taking in the free
show. This may have been one time Ripley wasn't nervous.
Here is a sample of Bob's prose that enchanted evening.

"In my travels to the Orient, I have always been fascinated
by the unexplainable miracles that the holy men of India per-
form. It has been one of my fondest hopes someday to present
one of these miraculous feats on my program. Tonight I have
the great pleasure of realizing this ambition, and in just a few
moments you will hear an eyewitness description of the most
famous of all the feats of the mystics of the Orient. From
India I have brought a mystic whose name is Kuda Bux. Tonight he will actually walk, barefoot, over a bed of flaming
coals . . ."

Ripley then went on to describe the pit across which Kuda
Bux was to walk, twenty-five feet long, four feet wide, and
four feet deep. Since early morning a fire had been burning
there, and it was now what Bob was pleased to call "a bed
of flaming coals." When Ripley left the studio, to cover the
time gap the orchestra played "I'm Gonna Lock My Heart"
and announcer Ben Grauer delivered the middle commercial
for Post's Bran Flakes.

Graham McNamee, one of the most breathless announcers
of his or any other day, a man who always sounded as if he
were announcing the end of the world, was at pitside, await-

ing the arrival of Ripley. Graham wasn't missing any bets, either. He took over after the middle commercial and described the pit also.

"But from where I am standing, all I can see of that pit is a mass of burning coals, red-hot coals that shine brightly in the night. From here I can feel the terrific heat that radiates from the pit, and ranged alongside are batteries of newsreel and newspaper cameramen making a picture record of this historic event. The fire has been burning since early morning, and more than five cords of oak firewood have been consumed to make this dense mass of burning coals which will form the searing carpet over which this Oriental mystic will make his barefoot walk. Bob Ripley has had engineers make temperature tests of the coals and the last reading was just over fourteen hundred degrees Fahrenheit. Even from here the heat is unbearable."

Graham then described Ripley's approach with as much reverence and awe as if he were Moses approaching through the divided waters of the Red Sea.

"The crowd is milling about now . . . the cameras are grinding . . . and o-ho! Here comes Bob Ripley. He has a police escort and he's getting nearer—he's fighting through the crowd—and here he comes!"

Ripley took over at this point and made the announcement that Kuda Bux was "completely cool and unruffled" and taking off his shoes and socks, that the doctors were about to examine his feet. The physicians were Dr. John Hudson Storer (Doug's father, by happy coincidence), the New York City Health Commissioner, Dr. John L. Rice, and Dr. Van Alstyne Cornell, a skin specialist, of the Fifth Avenue Hospital. The doctors pronounced Kuda Bux's feet to be normal, no signs of calluses or any other growth which might make them less sensitive to fire, and they had been washed to be sure there were no chemicals or any other substances on his feet to protect them.

With Ripley on one side of the pit and McNamee on the other, Kuda Bux strutted his stuff. Indeed, he hotfooted the length of the pit at such a rapid pace that the newsreel men screamed for him to do it over, which he did. There was another examination by the doctors, who found no scars or burns, normal body temperature, and nothing to indicate that he had been walking on fire.

Ripley was practically beside himself, calling it "the most amazing thing I have ever seen" and speaking of the "blazing inferno" and "amazing ordeal." Then he asked Kuda Bux how he had accomplished this "fantastic miracle."

"It is faith, Mr. Ripley. It is faith I have that allows me to do it," replied Kuda Bux, in one of the shortest curtain speeches in radio's history.

"Well, Kuda Bux, it must be faith," said Ripley, "because that fire was so hot that none of us here could get within three feet of it, yet you walked through it as easily as you would stroll down Fifth Avenue on a Sunday afternoon."

After a bit more of the same by Ripley, the show switched back to the studio, where Linda Lee, accompanied by B. A. Rolfe's orchestra, sang "A-Tisket A-Tasket," and Grauer delivered the closing commercial. Kuda Bux had had his hour in the sun, his walk on the coals.

This was the sort of stunt which pleased Ripley, which made radio worthwhile for him. This was an audio—indeed, a visual—demonstration of a "Believe It or Not," not mere documentation or a dry quote from a dusty encyclopedia. He loved the excitement, with the fire engines standing by, lest the fire from the pit consume all the stone and granite of Radio City, the blanket insurance policy for a million dollars taken from Lloyd's of London covering all contingencies from

8:00 A.M. to midnight. If Bob had any regrets over the show at all, it probably was that he himself hadn't been able to walk over the coals.

Since the Ripley show was based on offbeat material, it was obvious that the office should be something of a focal point for weird characters. Many unsolicited guests presented themselves there, confident that their story was just what Rip needed for his broadcast. He had a set rule that nobody, but nobody, should be tossed out of the office without a hearing.

A middle-aged man, neatly but not richly dressed, appeared one day and requested an interview. He told Rip and Storer he had something to sell, something which would put the Ripley show on front pages all over the country, perhaps all over the world, the next day, something which never had been done before over the air.

"You may have read, Mr. Ripley," began the visitor, who spoke calmly but earnestly, "that condemned prisoners frequently make arrangements to have their bodies sold to scientific schools after their execution. The money received for the cadaver goes to the family of the man."

Ripley nodded to show that he was familiar with this practice, and the visitor continued.

"Now, I would like to obtain some money, a fairly large amount, to provide for my family. If you will guarantee that my family will receive five thousand dollars, I will go on your show at any date you select and commit suicide over the air!"

There was a concerted gulp from Rip and Storer, and the latter backed away slightly to be in a better defensive position should the man become violent. Mistaking their silence for doubt, the visitor elaborated on his plans.

"I'd leave the *modus operandi* up to you, Mr. Ripley. As long as I am going to commit suicide, I don't care whether the script calls for me to shoot myself, hang myself, or take poison. You name it and I'll do it."

Ripley realized that the man was serious. He stuttered more than usual as he began to hedge, to mention that there might be some legal obstacles to such a performance, that he and his staff might be arrested as accessories. Each objection the man brushed aside by promising to sign waivers for any and all contingencies. The man was not to be put off.

Suddenly a light dawned on Rip. "No, sir," he said with more assurance than he had shown previously. "We just couldn't put you on the air to commit suicide. I'm not saying you haven't got an original idea, mind you, but it just wouldn't be practical."

"And why wouldn't it be practical?" the visitor demanded.

"You see," explained Ripley patiently, "our first show goes on in the studio at Eastern time, at eight o'clock. Then we have to go back on the air four hours later for the benefit of the Pacific Coast and other western stations. Now if you committed suicide on our first show, what could we do for the rebroadcast?"

The man took the explanation in understandably crushed silence and abruptly rose and stalked out of the office. Ripley and Storer just looked at each other, gasping great sighs of relief.

"At that, Doug," said Rip with a faraway look in his eyes, "it would have been a helluva show."

Ed Gardner, who was to achieve fame and fortune as Archie in "Duffy's Tavern," entered radio modestly as a director for the J. Walter Thompson agency, which at one time handled the Ripley account. Rip had discovered that there was an itinerant preacher operating in the Ozarks whose honest moniker was Santa Claus. Claus was the family name, and apparently his parents had a sense of humor, for they legally baptized their child Santa. It was Ripley's thought that the preacher would make an ideal guest for a program he had scheduled for Christmas night. Imagine introducing an honest-to-goodness Santa Claus on Christmas night! He told Storer to ferret out the preacher and arrange for him to come to New York.

The preacher wrote back that he would be glad to come to New York if transportation could be arranged and that he would arrive on Christmas Eve.

Christmas Eve afternoon in the offices of an advertising agency is like Christmas Eve afternoon in almost any office, only more so. So it was in the J. Walter Thompson agency. By three o'clock the office was deserted, except for two employees, the switchboard operator, who was getting time and a half, and Gardner, a young man with a purpose. His instructions were to wait for a phone call from the preacher, pick him up, and install him in a hotel.

The minutes went by in silence. About every half-hour Gardner would call the operator to see if there had been a message for him. There was none. After a couple of hours of waiting, Ed was beginning to feel the strain. He grabbed the phone again.

"Look," he said to the operator, "are you sure there haven't been any calls for me?"

"No, Mr. Gardner," said the operator, "none at all."

"You mean not a single call has come in in the last two hours?" persisted Ed.

"No business calls at all," said the girl firmly, and then added, "Only some nut who keeps calling about every five minutes saying he's Santa Claus. I just hang up on him. What drink will do to some people!"

Gardner broke all sprint records in getting to the switchboard. "When that guy calls again, give me the earphones,"

he told the somewhat astonished operator. Santa Claus called
and Ed spoke to him. Somewhat wearily Santa explained that
he was in Penn Station, had been there for a couple of hours,
and was rather amazed that a metropolis as large as New
York should have such poor phone service. "Every time I get
your number, I get disconnected," he told Ed.

Gardner told him not to move from the phone booth and
dashed over to pick him up. He proved to be a gem too,
with a flowing white beard, long white hair, and the general
air of benignity which one associated with Santa Claus. The
program was a huge success.

"Why didn't you tell the girl you were expecting a call from
Santa Claus?" somebody asked Gardner years later, when he
was relating the episode.

"On Christmas Eve?" snorted Ed. "She'd have walked right
out of the building or else called the cops."

Starting off on a new tack in 1940, Ripley committed several radio shows which would have been inevitably pronounced "spectaculars," had they come along in a later period
of electronics. They were the product of the nimble imagination of Douglas Storer. They were the product, too, of necessity. The war had closed off considerable portions of the
world, a blow to Ripley's chief gimmick and trade-mark—his
restless search for new stories, fresh oddballs, different ad-
ventures around which to build his burbling scripts.

Storer's idea was patriotically foolproof. Out of it came
Rip's "See America First" series. An examination of the warps,
woofs, and wonders of these shows reveal a corn-soaked
technique all but extinct now in radio. To the modern user of
the radio—accustomed to a steady fare of music, heady claims
to relief from pain, and news—they will seem to be fragments
from the scrolls of a lost rite.

Ladling "adventure" by the shovelful, Ripley roamed the

United States and as far into the outer world as Nassau, tensely reading his rattling scripts against backdrops that ranged from a hissing snake pit in Silver Springs, Florida, to an unprecedented meeting with the Duke of Windsor, then Governor of the Bahamas. His listeners heard this.

B. A. ROLFE

(the bandmaster and often straight man in these scripts)

"Well, ladies and gentlemen, Bob Ripley should be ready to speak to you now from the heart of Florida. Are you all ready up there? Then—take it away, Bob Ripley—in Silver Springs, Florida."

Ripley was indeed "ready up there." So was a sound-effects man and a curious ally, a dynamite expert. The script at this point called for "OPEN FULL WITH ALLIGATOR SOUNDS AND SUSTAIN UNTIL CUT ON CUE." The production problem was somewhat more complex, however. Alligators become considerably more amiable at lower temperatures, and such prevailed on this particular occasion. So they were roused to grumble, all the way from a nagging whine to a bull-voiced roar, by setting off dynamite charges in the immediate vicinity of their muddy couches. Once this had been attended to, and Rip had comprehended the sweep of the director's arm as a signal to start reading, the main event was under way.

RIPLEY

"This is Bob Ripley, speaking to you from the greatest Believe It or Not springs in the world—the famed Silver Springs, located just five miles east of Ocala, Florida. And don't be frightened by that noise you hear in the background. It is just the bellowing of the alligators, who are all excited by this broadcast from their homeland!"

(PAUSE HERE FOR SOUND)

"Would you like to listen to a real man-eating alligator when he is mad?"

(PAUSE FURTHER FOR SOUND: AD LIB ABOUT ALLIGATORS)

"Silver Springs is the largest flowing springs in the world. Nine hundred and seventy-five million gallons of crystal-clear water gushing up through the limestone rocks—enough, ladies and gentlemen, to provide five gallons a day for every man, woman, and child in the United States! The water at the springs here is so remarkably clear that you can see the bottom sixty feet below just as if there was no water at all. Because of the clarity of the water, Silver Springs has become the place where almost all underwater motion pictures are filmed.

"As I gaze below to the bottom of the springs, I can see the fish swim by in brilliant procession. I see the famed black bass . . . the bluefin dace . . . the comical catfish with chin whiskers . . . and the long, rakish garfish, known as the spotted leopard of Silver Springs. And here is a real 'Believe It or Not' of the water world: the giant shrimp, actually two feet long. Imagine that—a shrimp two feet long!

"Along the bottom of Silver Springs there are flower gardens under water. Blooming there I see the beautiful bridal flowers, and the foxtail, swaying like a greenish plume, and the fantastic underwater Christmas trees—fourteen feet high—and as the sunlight falls and the fish swim through and the glistening snails fall on the leaves, it looks like it is decorated for a visit from Saint Nick!

"More than half a million visitors a year come here to view this underwater fairyland from glass-bottomed boats.

"But of all the 'Believe It or Nots' I have found in Silver Springs, there is one that surpasses anything I have met in my twenty-five years of searching for the unusual. His name is Ross Allen, and to give you an idea of his courage—— Only two hours ago we went out with Colonel Toohey in his jungle boat down Silver River. And Ross Allen did something I never thought a man would do. As we cruised along, the ominous head of a ten-foot alligator appeared beside the boat. Ross Allen then actually dove onto the back of that alligator and clamped his hand over the mouth of the 'gator—which has, Believe It or Not, eighty wicked-looking teeth. Ross then wrapped his legs around that 'gator and conquered him. That's the man I want you to meet now. Ladies and gentlemen . . . Ross Allen."

ROSS

"Good evening . . ."

RIPLEY

"Ross, how did you conquer that alligator?"

ROSS

"I tired him out."

RIPLEY

"You tired him out?"

ROSS

"Yes. You've just got to understand them."

RIPLEY

"Well, Ross, that's a little detail I'll leave to you—understanding alligators. Here at Silver Springs, Ross Allen has the largest reptile institute in America. I have seen the four greatest snake farms in the world: in South Africa, Brazil, Honduras, and Siam. But I have never seen a man handle snakes as Ross Allen does. He is standing beside me now—still wet from his battle with the 'gator, and he is wearing nothing but his bathing suit. He is bare-armed, barelegged, and barefooted.

"Now we are standing in front of his largest snake pit here, and there are five hundred deadly poisonous snakes in there. Ross Allen will now go into that pit—bare-armed—barelegged, and barefooted, and actually *milk* a rattlesnake for you.

"It is necessary for me to go into that pit myself to tell you *how* he milks the rattler. But Ross gave me special snakeproof boots, and I'll walk through the snake pit with him."

(FADE IN SOUND OF RATTLERS AS RIPLEY AND ROSS GET INTO THE PIT)*

ROSS

"All ready Bob? Hear them rattling? They're ready for us! Now, up the ladder and over the side. Nervous, Bob?"

Ripley's script called for him to say, with as much dignity as he could summon and in as many words as he could read as he climbed over the retaining wall:

"Well, yes, I am. But after the man-eating sharks on the ocean bottom last week and a pitful of snakes this week, these 'Believe It or Not' programs will be the end of me yet. Maybe that's my knees rattling."

(FADE RATTLERS IN FULL)

Ripley's ad libbing from the pit cleared up a question which no doubt concerned millions of his listeners. The "milking" was pressing a rattler's venom into a goblet. It was a performance that warranted a curtain bow, but Ripley was through for the night as soon as he said, with understandable relief, "Take it away, B. A. Rolfe!"

At that, it was a letdown for Ripley, compared to the dress rehearsal of the night before. Just as he and Ross lowered themselves among the snakes on the trial run, every light in the area went out. The terror of that predicament was compounded by Ross, who roared, "Let's get the hell outa here!"

Investigation revealed that the short circuit was caused by muskrats who had been nibbling at a deliciously insulated main conduit for months, perhaps years, and bit into the cable itself just in time to imperil the life of Robert L. Ripley and the fiscal affairs of King Features Syndicate.

* The cold and drowsy snakes were roused into rattling good form by warming them suddenly with infrared lights.

Bob had a radio show that was subject to change without notice. In a day when much of the present-day magic in remote pickups and switch overs was unknown, Rip and Storer proceeded confidently where most radio engineers feared to tread. Ripley's show in connection with the Birmingham, Alabama, air show, on the night of May 31, 1940, was a case in point.

After a tribute to Royal Crown Cola as eloquent as one Lucius Beebe might address himself to listing the joys of a bottle of Krug '21, the show's announcer shouted:

"And here's that aggressive, alert, aggrandizing ambassador of arduous, augmented, animated argonauts of the air . . ."

Turned out to be Ripley he was talking about. Script fluttering anxiously, Bob plunged in.

RIPLEY

"Greetings, everyone, and welcome to the program tonight! This is Bob Ripley, speaking to you from the stage of the vast municipal auditorium in Birmingham, Alabama! This is a great night for Birmingham, for tomorrow the Tenth National Air Carnival opens and more than two hundred and fifty thousand people will gather here tomorrow and Sunday at Birmingham's million-dollar airport and watch a breath-taking exhibition of flying.

"Late in the program, for the first time ever on the air, we will attempt to present the thrilling parachute drop of twelve thousand feet, as daredevil Jack Huber leaps from a plane and falls, without his parachute, in a delayed drop, for ten thousand, five hundred feet, and then pulls his rip cord and the silvery puff of the parachute blossoms out and he sways gently to the ground. In this parachute jump, Jack Huber will actually *talk* to you with a small portable pack transmitter he will

be wearing . . . for the first time, describing his sensations as
he falls!"

That was the last mention of his star attraction for a considerable spell.

Around him now, and braced to undergo his interrogations,
fidgeted "a group of the most famous fliers in the world today."

They were indeed. Prodded by Ripley's questions, Jimmy
Mattern told of survival in Siberia after a crack-up. Roger
Q. Williams described a safe upside-down landing he had
made ("I sat the ship down in such a way that the wings
rested on the saplings along the side of the road and the fuse-
lage just cleared the road"). Major Leslie Arnold told of the
Army's harrowing first aerial circumnavigation of the world.
Jimmy Doolittle topped things off with a shy but hair-raising
account of how he outstunted a German rival pilot, although
both his legs were broken and in casts.

Then back to Huber—a man who must by that time have
developed certain reservations about the entire business.

RIPLEY

"Ladies and gentlemen. Now I shall present a 'Believe It or
Not' which has never been done on the air before. Just five
miles from where I am standing, at the million-dollar Birmingham airport, two planes are circling lazily in the night sky. One
of them is a small passenger sports plane, and in it is Jack Huber, a young man who will make a parachute jump of twelve
thousand feet—almost two and one half miles—and actually *describe* his sensations to you as he falls. Circling around this
smaller plane is a twenty-one-passenger luxury liner, piloted
by Major Alton Parker, and with him is our announcer, Maury
Farrell, who will describe the jump.

"Huber will jump, and then, for a dizzying, breath-taking two miles, he will fall at the rate of a hundred and sixty miles an hour, falling the first two miles in just one minute. Then, as he pulls his rip cord, in one second his speed will diminish from a hundred and sixty miles an hour to twenty miles an hour as his parachute blossoms out in the night air! I leave it to your imagination what that sudden stop from a hundred and sixty miles an hour to twenty miles an hour in one second does to the human body.

". . . In the giant plane accompanying Jack Huber's plane we have our announcer, Maury Farrell, and piloting the ship is Major Alton N. Parker . . . one of the most brilliant pilots in modern aviation! He was chosen by Admiral Byrd from three thousand pilots, and has flown far over both the North and South Poles with Admiral Byrd's expeditions! He is a member of the select One Million Mile Club of pilots—and in his plane, he is waiting now to talk to you. . . . I have special radio equipment here so that I can talk with him. . . . Come in, Major Parker . . . come in, Major Parker . . ."

PARKER

"Hello, Bob Ripley! This is Major Alton Parker, speaking to you from the TWA twenty-one-passenger DC-3 airliner, now cruising directly over the Birmingham airport."

RIPLEY

"You're coming in fine, Major Parker. Tell us—how is the wind up there?"

PARKER

"It might throw Jack Huber off a little in his judgment."

RIPLEY

"How is the night?"

PARKER

"Visibility fine . . . weather clear . . . looks like a good night."

RIPLEY

"What is your present height?"

PARKER

"Just over twelve thousand feet, Bob . . . but I see the other plane is signaling with its landing lights, so I'll get back to handling the ship and turn you over to Maury Farrell."

FARRELL

"Thank you, Major! Bob Ripley, this is Maury Farrell, and as Major Parker told you, we are now twelve thousand feet above the airport. The other ship is circling and we are circling with it. Jack Huber is waiting for us to light the signal flare before he jumps. The signal flare is released from the plane automatically when the pilot pushes a lever. It throws a blinding white light and is standard equipment for use in emergencies. Jack Huber is ready to jump, and, believe me, he has a man-sized job tonight. Jack has made many jumps before, but he has never made one weighed down by a twenty-pound pack transmitter strapped to his chest. It might make some difference in the fall . . . as he is used to making his free fall, and guiding himself with both arms outstretched, like a bird . . . but with that pack, he may not be able to keep his balance, and instead go tumbling over and over and over. . . . Now, we're circling his plane . . . we're in good position, and here goes the flare! When Jack sees it he will jump . . . and then count ten very slowly . . . and then . . . try to speak to you as he plunges through the night air, aiming at the tiny, glowing spot that is the airport. If there is any difficulty with his portable transmitter, I will again speak to you and describe this fall.

"Oh! I can see him now . . . standing up in his plane. He is ready to jump. His six lights are lighted, making him look like some weird man from Mars! He sees the flare now . . . AND THERE HE GOES! TAKE IT AWAY, JACK HUBER!"

(BRING UP SHRIEK OF WIND FOR 10 SECONDS)

(AFTER PAUSE: BRING IN JACK HUBER FALLING)

Things didn't work out quite that way. The airport officials informed Storer that if they turned on all the lights they'd blow the fuses—and Huber would have to settle for perimeter lights and a flare in the middle of the runway. The DC-3 "luxury liner" lost sight of the little plane in which Huber was riding. He jumped, not on the flare cue, but by looking at his watch and remembering that Storer had told him he'd probably jump during the twenty-third minute of the show.

If Huber said anything as he fell, it was drowned out by the wind whistling across the microphone Storer had built into the apparatus. Huber wore two chutes, and just as well. The first one ripped away. The second one worked, but, still, he hit the ground with a wallop that knocked the wind out of him. Storer sped to the landing point, at the edge of the field, and thought for a moment that he was dead. When it developed that he wasn't, he rushed him back to a field microphone. Ripley was on.

RIPLEY

". . . All I can say is, 'Believe It or Not.' Ladies and gentlemen, you have just heard, in his own words, Jack Huber's sensations as he made a twelve-thousand-foot parachute drop . . . almost two and a half miles over the Birmingham airport! Jack Huber fell at the terrific rate of a hundred and sixty miles an hour, for one minute, before opening his parachute to check his fall! Then . . . in one second . . . one muscle-tearing, agonizing second, he was slowed down from the speed of a hundred and sixty miles an hour to twenty miles an hour as his parachute blossomed and caught the night air! And I must say that I, for one, never heard a more thrilling description in my life. And in a few moments, we will switch back to the airport, when Jack himself will speak to you, to prove that he landed safely, and that all is well. I am sure tonight, Jack Huber has created a world's record in thrills . . . Believe It or Not!" (APPLAUSE)

Back at the airport, Storer had propped the winded parachutist up against a mike.

"I don't know what to say," Huber told him.

"Don't get nervous," Storer said. "Just say something like, 'Well, Bob Ripley, here I am safely on the ground, and it sure was an interesting jump.'"

The cue came from Ripley downtown, and, dutifully, Huber said, "Well, Bob Ripley, here I am safely on the ground, and it sure was an interesting jump."

He was off the air now. Storer took him by the arm. "We're going down to the auditorium now so you can take a bow to the people in the audience."

"O.K.," said Huber, "but take it easy. Speeding makes me nervous."

The year 1941 was one to remember, filled with surprises to Rip and his audiences. The Duke of Windsor had turned down repeatedly the invitations by U.S. networks to use their facilities for anything he wished to say. To make the invitations more palatable, he was promised that if he did appear, there would not be the faintest hint of commercialism involved. Storer signed him up for Ripley's Royal Crown Cola show by dint of a piece of superb salesmanship. Two British merchant mariners had just reached the Bahamas in December 1941, after a dramatic seventy-day-and-night battle with the Atlantic. Their vessel was little more than a rowboat, and they were the two who survived the incredible ordeal, out of an original company of seven which took to the little boat after their ship was torpedoed. Rip's researchers saw in this a greater feat than the voyage of Bligh.

Storer arrived in Nassau ten days before the broadcast, dreaming of a bigger show than the presentation of the two survivors. His first target was Sir Harry Oakes, soon to be the victim of a macabre murder, which still has not been solved. He spent several days with Oakes, complimenting the multimillionaire on his extensive plans for a Greater Nassau. It was such a good buttering up job that the vain and somewhat eccentric Oakes (who had literally struck gold in Canada years before, when thrown off a train for stealing a ride) paved Doug's way to a meeting with H.R.H. the Duke, in lonely and remote exile with the woman he loved. Storer briskly invited him to appear on Rip's show, in his capacity as head of the British Red Cross in the area. Ripley kept telling Doug, "You're crazy, he'll never do it." The clincher was Storer's suggestion that it would be a grand opportunity for the Duke to pay tribute to the unsung men of the Merchant Marine everywhere.

"Certainly," the Duke said.

Storer spent much of the next week on the telephone. The agency involved in the Ripley show—Batten, Barton, Durstine & Osborn—took a thoroughly dim view of the Duke's appearance. So did CBS. They were fearful that His Royal Highness might say something on the American air which would offend isolationists who drank or might consider drinking Royal Crown Cola or automatically label CBS as interventionist-minded by his very appearance! Such were the times.

When Storer had made both the agency and the network understand that Ripley had his star and would use him, come hell or Hitler, the dissenters asked Storer to write the Duke's speech for him and water it down to transparency. Storer refused.

Inevitably, His Royal Highness learned of this tempest, through his government's phone monitors. He called Storer and shyly offered to withdraw—"If it is going to be embarrassing to anyone." Storer reassured him—and the show went off splendidly. The Duke's salute to the two survivors and their peers, past and present, was warmly eloquent. At a soiree later in the evening, the survivors' little boat was raffled off for the Red Cross. The bidding became quite spirited from two challengers on opposite sides of the room, Sir Harry Oakes and a woman he could not see. Finally Oakes topped his stubborn rival—who turned out to be Lady Oakes. He hadn't recognized her voice.

The same year saw Rip's show touch two bottoms—the one at Marineland, Florida, and the bed of the Colorado River on the floor of Grand Canyon.

Both were samples of a rougher day in radio.

At Marineland the gimmick was the milking—actually lactic, this time—of a big cow porpoise. The willingly co-operative mammal was dredged up from the pool depths on a kind of latticework stretcher, via derrick, and Ripley went to work on one of her teats for the benefit of a camera crew shooting a film sequence. There was some difficulty reaching the teat. An attendant pulled out a knife and cut one of the canvas "slats" of the stretcher. In doing so he also cut the porpoise, who bled on Ripley's bathing suit.

That much out of the way, Ripley put on a diver's helmet, packed his oxygen, and was lowered to the bottom of the deep pool, along with a Marineland expert. Though he could not swim a stroke, he was completely unmindful of the danger involved. Indeed, he was still vilely cursing his script writer for not having provided him with "some ad libs to say down there."

The professional diver did not like the looks of things. Something was brewing among Marineland's sharks. They weren't taking the mullets off the pointed stick he was teaching Ripley how to use. Then they began circling the pair, as if closing in. And indeed they were. They had picked up the scent of blood on Rip's suit, and it promised a better meal than mullet. One shark then charged, collided with Ripley, and knocked him to the seat of his pants. The alarmed pro ordered both men pulled up instantly.

The next night the lashed script writer humbly approached Rip with a few sheets of extemporaneous remarks. Ripley, a terrible tyrant with his help, knocked the pages from the man's hand. "You imbecile!" he roared, oblivious to all but his rage. "How do you expect me to read underwater!"

The smashing, crashing trip down a section of the Colorado River's rapids was made without Rip as an active participant. He described the harrowing event from shore and bowed to the two men in the boat to give the more soulful account. One of these was especially articulate. He was a big, athletic fellow from Phoenix who came in answer to Storer's call for an announcer from the station that would feed the show to the network. Rip disapproved of him on sight. "Why didn't they send a little guy?" he grumbled. "This fellow will sink the boat."

Actually, the "announcer" was the operator of a local department store which spent a great deal of money advertising on that station. When he heard of the Ripley show's need for such talent, he demanded that he be sent on the job. He was a young man named Barry Goldwater.

CHAPTER IX

Ripley's Golden Age

THE decade of the 1930s, when the United States was in the worst of its depression, was Bob Ripley's "Golden Age." Along with his success in radio, he was coining money as an entrepreneur (of "Odditoriums" and traveling freak shows); as a performer (in movie shorts, in vaudeville, and on the lecture circuit); as an author (of the *Believe It or Not* books); and, of course, as the originator and executor of the most successful of all syndicated newspaper features. During this decade also he hit the peak as a public figure—a success epitomized when he was made the subject of cartoons in *The New Yorker, Esquire,* the *Saturday Evening Post,* and other magazines.

With all this Ripley became, as the famed columnist O. O. McIntyre pointed out, "the first millionaire cartoonist." The range of his interests necessarily made him a businessman, but never a particularly adept one. He incorporated "Believe It or Not" in 1931, and the minutes of the early corporate meetings show that he was more than a little confused. He couldn't make up his mind what to do about the stock. He had turned over to the corporation all his trade-marks in return for stock—a fairly simple transaction, it would seem—but this stock he was constantly shuffling and redistributing among himself and the other, nominal stockholders. At each meeting he would apportion it differently. Finally he settled the matter to his own satisfaction, doing what was expected—keeping the lion's share himself—and thereafter there were only a few corporate meetings.

Ripley didn't have to be a particularly skilled businessman because he had so much going for him—the unrivaled attraction of his "Believe It or Not" idea, his own acute sense of self-promotion, and the helping hands of others. He could make money by any means through which he could transmit the idea to a willing and eager public, and he could afford the waste that stemmed from lack of planning and, sometimes, irrationality.

After the immediate success of his first book, a second edition was turned out in 1931, and in 1934 the first two were combined, with a few changes, variations, and deletions, into a third edition. Together they sold considerably more than a million copies. (Those three were the last Ripley actually had a hand in, but eight more were brought out after his death by Doug Storer, as president of Believe It or Not.)

Anyone who saw the incredibly awkward Ripley in the early days of radio would find it hard to believe that he would dare step up on a stage or before a movie camera. He did both, and although, artistically, he left an enormous amount to be desired, he made money. In 1930 he appeared in a series of movie shorts for Vitaphone, talking about and showing some of his oddities, and later did other, similar series for Warner Brothers and Twentieth Century-Fox, as a result of Storer's inspiration. All in all there were more than fifty of these shorts, and Rip's take from them was well up in the hundreds of thousands of dollars.

While the movie camera held terror for Rip, some of his stage experiences were absolutely nightmarish. In 1931 he set out on a vaudeville tour of the East. He was doing four shows a day, essentially talks illustrated with slides. The *pièce de résistance* of his talk was his version of how he came to draw the famous "Marching Chinese" cartoon, after which a stooge in the gallery would shout, "Darn clever, these Chinese!" That will give some idea not only of the nature of the show but of the tensile strength of man's patience in those days before the atom had been split. On the first day of the tour, in Boston, Rip almost didn't get away with the show at all. After the first performance he was under such a strain that in his dressing room he broke down in uncontrollable sobs. He did improve; he acquired some confidence; and he was able to finish the tour. And this was one more example of the mighty effort he was capable of expending to overcome his shyness.

On the vaudeville and lecture circuits, as elsewhere, his shyness marched hand in hand with self-promotion. He purchased a luxurious chauffeur-driven foreign limousine, an Isotta-Fraschini, to take him from one vaudeville date to another. It would be parked in front of the theater at which he was appearing, and it would draw bigger crowds than a sideshow barker.

Overcoming his shyness on such an occasion frequently required more than the exercise of will on Ripley's part. He found strength in one hundred-proof alcohol mixed with grapefruit juice and in similar combinations. Sometimes he got more spirit than he bargained for. Once in Bronxville, New York, appearing at a Boy Scout benefit, he lurched unceremoniously off the edge of the stage and was helped back on by startled patrons of the event.

One of Ripley's early lectures was delivered in a small Ohio town. The local vaudeville house was done over for the occasion, with a large green baize cloth covering the orchestra pit where the musicians were wont to fiddle and tootle when the theater was playing host to the two-a-day shows of that era.

Ripley felt the need of a stimulant to combat his stage fright, and fortified himself accordingly. As he stepped on-stage, he peered, woebegone, into the glare of the footlights. Shading his eyes with his hand, Bob advanced past the foot-lights to see if there really was an audience hidden out there in the Stygian darkness of the orchestra. As soon as he stepped over the glaring footlights and onto the green baize, he plunged to the bottom of the empty orchestra pit.

The nervous lecturer, entangled in the cloth and in the blackness of the empty pit, struggled more like Laocoön than Burton Holmes. When he finally disencumbered himself of the blanketing cloth, he discovered that there was only one way out of the pit, an exit under the stage which led to the street. To get back into the theater he had to walk around the block, purchase a ticket from the astonished peroxide blonde in the cashier's cupola, walk down the aisle, and clamber onto the stage. The audience applauded vigorously, on the assumption that a collector of oddities would naturally open his lecture on a novel note. Ripley saw nothing comical in his mishap. Bob never had a great sense of humor, only a sense of the unusual.

If Max Schuster could be credited with launching Ripley in the book business, Joe Connolly with shooting him to the top as a syndicated cartoonist, and Doug Storer with carrying him over the shoals in radio, such credit as may be due for making Ripley an entrepreneur of freak shows goes to a fabu-lous character named C. C. Pyle.

A slim, dapper gent with a wispy Chaplinesque mustache, Pyle was a sports promoter in the tradition of Tex Rickard, but with a difference: Rickard devoted himself entirely to the promotion of prize fights, preferably for the heavyweight championship. Pyle promoted wherever there was a loose dollar. Before he met Ripley, Pyle had, among many other ventures, introduced Harold (Red) Grange to professional football, and earned a considerable fortune for both of them. After Ripley, Pyle promoted a cross-country marathon called the Bunion Derby and promoted professional football at the Yankee Stadium. His initials eventually came to stand for "Cash and Carry."

Pyle was fresh out of cash in 1933, along with most other Americans. Chicago, in its customary mood of ebullience and optimism, opened a fair of truly mammoth proportions on its lake front and grandiloquently entitled it "A Century of Progress." Pyle, an instinctive carnival man, was drawn to the fair and, deciding that he had to have something original to promote, contacted Ripley for a "Believe It or Not" exhibition. All Rip's advisers warned him against the venture, but Bob, with his rapier intuition when a buck was involved, decided to go along with Pyle.

Under the corporate title of "International Oddities," Pyle got Ripley to open at the Century of Progress. Through a character of the same promotional stripe as himself, a Colonel Clint Finney, the live exhibits were collected. The exhibit itself was called "Ripley's Believe It or Not Odditorium." Blowups of some of Rip's more startling cartoons were exhibited, but, with all due respect to Ripley, the artist, it was the living oddities who carried the day.

Despite the pessimistic attitude of his friends, Ripley's show in Chicago in 1933 and 1934 was an unmitigated success. At two bits for children and forty cents for adults, the exhibition drew $1,100,000 in eight months. Only the "Streets of Paris" outdrew it, and that was a multi-exhibit at which first beer and then—in the second year of the exposition—whisky could be purchased.

Ripley's success in Chicago opened an entire new avenue

to him, thanks to Pyle—not only a source of income but a sort of added attraction for his syndicated feature and his radio shows. He opened another Odditorium at the Texas Centennial Exposition in Dallas in 1936, then one at the Golden Gate Fair in San Francisco, and another at San Diego. All were money-makers and all were contributors to the Ripley legend.

The live exhibits at Ripley's Odditoriums were not as unusual as his cartoon material, but still were bizarre enough to send normal citizens shrieking into the night. Perhaps the greatest tribute that can be given to them is to say that Rip was satisfied.

Some of the exhibits did double duty by appearing on Rip's weekly radio show. Only one was a disappointment, John Tio, a talking parrot who was supposed to speak better English than his master. He imitated Eddie Cantor, Bing Crosby, and the Mills Brothers. At the Odditorium he was fluent, but he chose to remain mute when on the Ripley radio show. Pained, Rip considered eating him.

Among those featured in these Ripley shows were a pair of boys known as the "Upside-Down Twins" who danced on their hands with bells on their arms and also boxed that way, as well as Julius Shuster, who could hold twenty billiard balls in one hand. He was modestly billed as the "Man with the Million Dollar Hands."

There was nothing in these exhibitions that couldn't be seen in an ordinary side show—the usual collection of physical freaks. What made them a drawing card was the magic of the Ripley name and the unusual term for the exhibit, "Odditorium."

Ripley hated the use of the term "freaks" and had a standing order that any of his employees using the word should be summarily dismissed. He preferred to think of these pranks of nature as "oddities" and insisted that everybody else within his hearing do the same.

It was another of Rip's many quirks, such as his insistence that everything around him be original, including such a utilitarian object as a wastebasket. Quite possibly his aversion to the word "freaks" stemmed from his own inordinate pride. Anybody, from Phineas Taylor Barnum on down, could have a freak show, but only Ripley could have an Odditorium. Actually, the one distinctive feature of Ripley's exhibitions, his blown-up cartoons, went virtually unnoticed as the spectators drank in visions of the fat lady and the sword swallower.

Some of the Ripley exhibits were fairly gruesome, even by side-show standards, whether they were called freaks or oddities. One such was Dagomarr Rochmann, whom Rip claimed he had discovered in Switzerland at a time when American college students were making headlines by swallowing goldfish, instead of crowding, en masse, into phone booths.

Rochmann, for reasons best known to himself, preferred to be billed as "the Great Waldo" and he daily demonstrated at the Odditorium what Ripley chose to call "his remarkable gastronomic achievement." Waldo would gulp down a swimming goldfish from a glass of water and then regurgitate it into an aquarium after some seconds in his stomach, still swimming, thus neatly reversing Jonah.

The live goldfish, however, was just a tidbit for Waldo, Ripley was careful to explain. The *pièce de résistance* was to swallow a lemon whole and bring it back again. This was a carny spieler's delight. "Watch it disappear!" the spieler would chant like an auctioneer. "Going, going, gone!"

While Waldo was bringing back the lemon, the barker was in sheer ecstasy. "This really is a very dangerous thing to attempt," he would gravely inform the crowd. "As you can see, when the lemon is forced back up the throat, it shuts off

Waldo's windpipe. His face turns red—from the effort and the shutting off of his wind. At times, when he attempts this feat without being in tiptop condition, the pressure of the lemon against Waldo's windpipe has caused him to fall on the stage in a dead faint."

Waldo must have been in tiptop shape at all times, for nobody around the show ever recalled him fainting, although his final act—the dessert, so to speak, of his gastronomical performance—could, and did, cause fainting among the spectators.

"College boys over here have made headlines by swallowing goldfish," said the spieler. "Now you will see what college boys in Switzerland swallow—live white mice."

Having delivered this calumny on the mountain republic, the barker would explain how Waldo would blow smoke on the mouse to quiet it. "The quiet mouse goes down easily," he chanted, "and Waldo smiles like the cat that swallowed the canary. Another puff of the cigarette is the signal for the mouse to come back into daylight, absolutely unharmed by his trip into Waldo's amazing stomach."

The mouse may have been unharmed but many of the spectators weren't themselves for days afterward.

Among other Odditorium attractions was a Dr. Mayfield, who shaved himself with a blazing blowtorch, later turned the torch on his unprotected eyeball, and finally put the torch directly into his mouth, extinguishing the flame with his tongue.

Ripley was particularly pleased with the Great Omi, whom he described as "the most remarkable-looking person I have seen in traveling to two hundred and one different countries." Omi, according to Rip, had been a major in the British Army, serving in the Desert Camel Corps with Lawrence of Arabia. Like some of the other live exhibits, Rip had the Great Omi on his radio show, something only Ripley would have thought of, since Omi's claim to fame was that he was tattooed from head to foot, something for which the radio audience had to accept Bob's word.

"Omi is a native of Great Britain," announced Ripley on the air, "and after the war decided to decorate his body in the manner of the ancient natives of the British Isles. It was the custom for the prehistoric Britons to paint themselves with a substance known as 'blue woad.' It was applied in weird designs in elaborate ceremonies. Omi, however, is unlike his ancient forebears because he can't wash off his design. He has had it permanently tattooed into his skin. From the top of his head to the soles of his feet, his entire body is covered with this unique blue pattern.

"Nine years were required to complete the intricate job. A recording device attached to the tattoo needle showed that fifteen million stabs of the needle were required to put the design on his head alone. More than five hundred million stabs were required to cover the rest of his body. This imperishable pattern was made with forty-year-old Chinese ink.

"Note how different the design is from that customarily used in tattooing," Ripley urged his baffled listeners. "The symmetry of the pattern was especially designed to fit the contours of Omi's face—even the ears are tattooed. Note also how close to his eyes the tattooing needle worked."

People who drove railroad spikes into their nostrils, who lifted substantial weights attached to their eyelids, who swallowed lighted neon tubes eighteen inches long, and who chewed electric bulbs and razor blades—all were part of the Ripley Odditorium. Rip also had inanimate objects, such as the shoes of the "Alton Giant," one Robert Wadlow, who supposedly grew to a height of eight feet, seven inches; a shrunken human head; an embalmed rooster with a tail

On Nanking Road, Shanghai, Ripley demonstrates China's postwar inflation; his armful of Chinese money equals only one U.S. dollar. A few months later, the Communists took over the city.

Ripley rides the surf in a Hawaiian outrigger at Honolulu.

Eric Sevareid and French engineer Bunau-Varilla broadcasting from Paris on Ripley's program.

Ripley helping Ross Allen take venom from rattlesnakes during a broadcast from Silver Springs, Florida.

Ripley "milking" a porpoise at Marineland, Florida, for Fox Movietone News.

Tapscott and Widdicombe, only survivors of a British tanker torpedoed off the coast of Africa during World War II, were interviewed by Ripley after being washed ashore in the Bahamas seventy-one days later.

Bob Ripley and Senator Barry Goldwater on the trail to the bottom of Grand Canyon to broadcast from the Colorado River.

Ripley broadcasting from the bank of the Colorado River. Doug Storer is directing Ripley, Hazel is timing the script, and Doug Ripley holds the lantern for his famous brother.

twelve feet long; a scold's bridle; a chastity belt; and the inevitable picture of the Last Supper painted on the head of a pin.

A presentation that had been made to Vice-President John Nance Garner was one of the inanimate exhibits. It was an outsized gavel, made of wood, which weighed two hundred and fifty pounds. Ripley billed it as "the world's largest gavel." He also could have called it, without fear of contradiction, "the world's most useless gift."

One of Rip's live exhibits, who doubled in as a radio performer on the Ripley show, then under Royal Crown sponsorship, was Bill Hajak, who was, of all things, a marathon pianist. Hajak opened the Broadway Odditorium show in 1939, starting out on his ivory-tickling marathon, and the next week, Ripley's show from CBS picked him up there, now with 168 consecutive hours to his credit, if credit is the word. A week later, playing his three hundred and thirty-sixth consecutive hour on the "Believe It or Not" show, Hajak was informed, more or less simultaneously, that he had just set a world record for continuous piano playing and also had become the father of a baby girl. He promptly stopped playing and dashed off to the hospital for a peek at his new daughter.

Somewhere between his successful shows at the Century of Progress in Chicago in 1933–34 and the Texas Centennial Exposition in Dallas in 1936, Ripley acquired the lifelike image of the Japanese artist, Hananuna Masakichi, the figure with which Ripley used to startle visitors, first at Bion and later at his Central Park West apartment. The image is mentioned again here only because of a note Ripley used in the publicity for the Texas Centennial, in which it was stated, "The teeth are his own." This could be possible, of course, but if so, it was a vain sacrifice upon the altar of verisimilitude, since the mouth of the figure was closed.

After his success at the expositions in Chicago, Dallas, San Francisco, and San Diego, it was his intention to open at the New York World's Fair in Flushing Meadows. Complications which neither Ripley nor the director of the fair, Grover A. Whalen, seemed able to surmount prevented the Odditorium from being among the attractions nestling in the shadow of the Trylon and Perisphere when the fair opened. One of the complications was that John Hix, creator of "Strange as It Seems," and as close to a rival as Rip ever had, had staked out a prior claim.

Colonel Finney, who had helped Ripley assemble live exhibits for the Chicago exposition, was on hand again to corral the unusual but seemed to lose interest when he learned the Odditorium was to be staged on city streets instead of a fairground. He did, however, help get Rip started.

For the New York Odditorium Ripley selected, in lieu of Flushing Meadows, the site of the old Hollywood restaurant, where Nils T. Granlund (NTG) used to trot out a line of show girls as lovely as the city had ever seen. It was owned and operated by Ripley, Bob Hyland, his accountant, and a third partner who had invested heavily.

It was an abysmal flop, the only failure, businesswise, Ripley ever was connected with. The partner kept things hot for Rip and Hyland with threats of lawsuits. Bob was worried for a long time about this, and was furious with Hyland, whom he blamed, unjustly, for mismanagement. The bald truth of the matter was that none of them had had any experience operating exhibits. All they knew was that the professionals who had run the shows for them in the past had made money.

Douglas Ripley, a liability to the Odditorium through most of its Broadway run, was an asset to Rip on one occasion, perhaps the only positive contribution he ever made to his elder brother's welfare. It certainly was the only time the younger Ripley ever was able to capitalize on his own thirst. When the creditors outnumbered the customers and a man from the marshal's office showed up with foreclosure papers, Doug, so the story goes, was told to "take the man out and buy him a drink and stall him off." Young Ripley accepted these orders like the greatest of soldiers. He did his job so nobly, and so completely, that neither he nor the man with the legal papers could stand. Meanwhile, a van backed up and most of Ripley's treasures were loaded into it and hauled off to the safety of his Mamaroneck hideout.

The Odditorium opened with a big bang at a private party and preview on July 12, 1939, a sizzling-hot night. It closed, under the sheriff's guns, in 1940, just in time for Ripley to reopen during the second year of the World's Fair in Flushing Meadows, this time with professional exhibitors doing the job. Despite the fact that World War II was engulfing most of Europe, and visitors to the fair fell off considerably, Ripley did a sensational business there—all the more remarkable, as Hix's "Strange as It Seems," with larger attendence at the fair in 1939, couldn't make a go of it.

There is no telling how well Ripley might have done had he been able to open from scratch at Flushing Meadows in 1939. He miscalculated in thinking that the visitors who came to New York by the millions in 1939 for the World's Fair would also look in on his Broadway Odditorium. When the fair visitors returned to midtown Manhattan, they had already had their fill of side shows and fringe entertainment. Now they were looking for something different, the legitimate theater, a first-run film at one of the bigger movie palaces or a name restaurant where they might glimpse a celebrity or two.

Although the Broadway Odditorium was not a financial success, there was at least one New Yorker on whom it exerted a magnetic pull. H. Allen Smith, then a rising young humorist on the New York *World-Telegram*, was a visitor and related his experiences there in the first of his best-selling books, *Low Man on a Totem Pole*.

One "Professor" Alexander Meyer, who was a marathon rocker, fascinated Smith. The "Professor," whose cultural achievement was to set a world record for rocking in a *straight* chair, was observed by Smith—"swinging his stalwart torso back and forth in the Broadway window of Ripley's Odditorium, completing the 2,963,021st bend of his engagement in that window.

"I had stopped in," continued Smith, "to see a young woman at the Odditorium eat a razor blade. She was the same girl who played the part of the headless woman in one of the establishment's more frightful side shows. When she wasn't in the chair, minus her head, she was off at another end of the hall using her head to eat razor blades.

"I was heading for the Broadway exit of the Odditorium when my eye fell upon a contrivance in a glass case standing near the door. It was a tall glass case and on one of its shelves, level with my head, was a chastity belt. Two middle-aged women were studying it when I came up and I heard one of them say, 'I think it's a harness for a goat.'"

The Broadway exhibition was a nightmare from start to finish. Doug Ripley was on the sauce and made it pay off only that one night when he distracted the bailiffs. He quarreled constantly with a young student working in the Odditorium, taking care of the "stiffs"—as those who faint at such shows are known in carny lingo.

Rip and Hyland were barking at each other continually, Ripley blaming Hyland for getting him into the mess in the first place. The whole thing was losing money rapidly—the partner's mostly—and that worthy was pretty unhappy about it and highly articulate in his dismay.

When the corporation went into bankruptcy in 1940, Ripley was one of the foremost creditors, but the third partner also lost heavily, and threatened suit against Ripley, Hyland, and Doug Ripley. Ripley lost about $95,000 in the venture.

Ripley brooded about the failure for months, and not merely because he regretted his financial loss. He worried about the possible lawsuit and was fearful that the whole story of the flop would be known to the public. He felt that fate had dealt him a double blow, in the two places in which he was most sensitive, his pocketbook and his pride.

When the Odditorium was firmly established at Flushing Meadows in 1940 and a distinct hit, Ripley's spirits revived. Strangely enough, he felt somewhat put out that not as many people fainted at his horrendous side shows in New York as had fainted in Chicago. In *The New Yorker* magazine profile he made a rather morose comment about this aspect of his exhibition.

"In Chicago, we used to have about a hundred people faint a day," said Rip, "and we had six cots put aside to take care of the 'stiffs.' Here we only have three and hardly ever do we get more than twenty faintings in any one day, unless it's a real hot one. Do the people here think they're more sophisticated or something?"

Since sixty per cent of the people—in Chicago, San Francisco or New York—was composed of out-of-town visitors, Ripley's complaint seemed rather academic. It easily could have been that, with a war raging in Europe, the sensitivity of the common man had been dulled. This was an explanation Ripley never accepted. He just couldn't see a war, even such a frightful one as was being waged at the time, making spectators callous to his "oddities."

Ripley, for all the almost paternal pride he took in his live exhibits, visited his Odditorium rarely. He showed up on open-

ing night and then might make one or two visits each suc-
ceeding month. Even when he had some of the oddities
appear on his radio show, as he frequently did, he rarely
studied their act, whether it was swiveling the head around at
a complete one-hundred-eighty degree angle or holding five
golf balls in the mouth while carrying on a conversation. He
depended on Storer to make the selections most likely to hor-
rify on his radio shows.

Through the NBC Artists' Service, Ripley booked several
of his live exhibits throughout the United States and Canada.
The first unit opened in Montreal in June 1936, and then
went on to Boston and other cities throughout the United
States. Bob didn't accompany these shows, or act as M.C.
even on their opening nights. He simply kept his live exhibits
working between the unveilings of his various Odditoriums.
The units were billed as "Ripley's Strange People in Person."
It was a title which would have fitted most of the guests at
the house parties he gave at Bion, Central Park West, or,
later, at Palm Beach.

None of the units that traveled for Ripley under the NBC
aegis was particularly spectacular. They consisted at various
times of Jeannie, a midget comedienne, with her "quintu-
plets"—five gals who weighed better than three hundred
pounds apiece; of Clarence Willard, a man who grew before
your eyes. The double-jointed Willard could stretch out and
add six inches to his height.

In addition to the usual girl acrobats and male mental mar-
vels, these NBC units of Ripley's contained something of a
smash finish. A man by the name of Frank Allen was frozen
into a cake of ice at the outset of the show, and then, for the
grand finale, brought back onstage and chopped out of the
ice. Bob thought it added an "original touch."

Ripley, one of the greatest cartoon artists of his age and

one of the very first original radio performers, came closer to perpetuating himself as a side-show producer and carnival arranger than through any of his natural talents.

Rush Jerome supplied Bob with many of his wackiest live exhibits, going so far as to dig up a one-legged tap dancer. They ranged from Billygoat Mandy, a character who could butt anybody senseless, to Bozo, a mind-reading dog. Ripley, for the most part, found them all charming.

Perhaps the outstanding characteristic of the Ripley Odditoriums, including the grand floperoo on Broadway, was the industry and unfailing good nature of the performers. They worked their acts constantly, it seemed, and wherever you looked, someone was chewing glass, sucking in his gut to show his spine, screeching bird imitations, lifting iron dumbbells with his eyelids, or simply showing off a tattooed hide decorated like a drunk's Easter egg.

The performers just loved being freaks, much as Rip abhorred the word. They were happy to show off their many talents, and the audience seemed equally happy to be observing their peculiarities. Although they worked hard and willingly, and had undoubtedly taken years to develop and perfect their macabre skills, theirs was not a rewarding profession. The top attractions seldom received more than $100 a week. Their side money, from the sale of autographed postcards, wouldn't keep a normal person eating for a week, even though he ate only electric bulbs.

Ripley, who was used to receiving mail on the grand scale, had to hire two extra mail clerks after the success of his first Odditorium in Chicago. Some of the acts which didn't make the grade were equally as interesting, or at least equally as unusual, as those who won their "R" for Ripley. It was a little disconcerting to Bob, aloof as he was from the common herd, to discover that there were so *many* freaks in America.

Every proud mother of every little freaklet wrote to press her suit. None seemed to think of the embarrassment it might cause her little darling, or the future traumas which might be induced by the public display of physical disfigurations. To quote Jimmy Durante, "Everybody want[ed] to get into the act."

The number of trick piano players in the country startled Ripley. There were pianists who played wearing boxing gloves, or with their toes, or while standing on their heads.

Contortionists seemed to be without number and without regard for age or sex. From three to sixty-three, they hopefully submitted pictures to Ripley, all smiling with suffused and strained faces while sitting on their chins.

There was an Alaskan Indian who claimed to be able to blow a sustained note on a trombone for two and a half minutes and an Eskimo who claimed to have a Malemute which had its furry paws singed by descending into a volcano. There was a man who claimed to be able to make beautiful music—Rachmaninoff's *Prelude*—playing on the leaves of trees and plants, and a woman who said she could jump rope for hours uninterruptedly while wearing roller skates.

The extra secretaries were both dazzled and nauseated by the volume and character of the mail from those who volunteered to exhibit their talents under the Ripley banner, people who were willing to submit in public to be nailed to a board or to have their lips sewed together. It all may have been art for art's sake, but it was hard on the normal stomach.

Only Ripley remained undismayed by the character of his mail. "The supply is really inexhaustible, isn't it?" he observed, pleased as a character out of Charles Addams.

It was, too.

Whatever Ripley may actually have thought of the freaks, he must have recognized that they contributed mightily not only to his income but to his fame. At the big public dinners that would be arranged for Ripley on his return from foreign lands—or on anniversaries of one type or another—Joe Connolly would slap Ripley on the back and reassure him, "Don't worry, Turkey [his nickname for everybody], we'll make a big man out of you yet." He knew and Rip knew that Bob was firmly ensconced as a "big man." The pages of the most important magazines testified to that, and to the link of Ripley's name with the freakish and bizarre.

As a sample, a cartoon by E. Simms Campbell in the October 1937 *Esquire* showed a lavishly endowed secretary and a bug-eyed boss telling a colleague, "My wife hired her for me—I phoned Ripley about it." Another cartoon depicted a man seated in a reception room with his hat in his lap and a geranium plant growing out of his head. There was no caption, but the name on the door leading to the inner office read: "Ripley's Believe It or Not." An *Esquire* cartoon of November 1940 showed a man and woman at the breakfast table. The woman was normal but the man had six arms and hands and two of them were holding an envelope. The caption read: "Letter from Robert L. Ripley. Wonder what he wants?"

Ripley continued generating his own publicity, largely by travel, during this prewar period. Not a year passed without some foreign expedition. After the Russian voyage there was Central and South America in 1934 and 1935; Europe, Africa, and India in 1936 (with a Joe Connolly welcome-home dinner for fifteen hundred persons in the Waldorf-Astoria main ballroom and a menu written in fifteen languages and ranging from soup to nuts); Alaska in 1937; a twenty-four-thousand-mile junket across two continents in 1938—from New York to Cairo and back, via the Cape of Good Hope and Buenos Aires;

fifteen thousand miles by air, eight thousand by ship, and a thousand by camel, auto, donkey, train, and horse.

A Ripley trip to Central America and the Caribbean over the Christmas holidays in 1938 was wild even by Ripley's standards. He had made arrangements to meet B. A. Rolfe and the band leader's wife, Edna, and was waiting for them when their cruise ship arrived in Haiti.

"He was simply bubbling over with enthusiasm," Mrs. Rolfe recalls. "He said that Doug Storer had just telephoned from New York to say that Coca-Cola was going to be their radio sponsor for the following season. All the publicity devices were put in motion—there were pictures of B.A. and Rip toasting each other in Coca-Cola, climbing up the mountain to the Citadel to drink Coca-Cola, feeding it to babies and the natives."

Ripley and his companions were Coca-Cola happy until they arrived back in New York, and encountered a sudden sobering up from Storer. He explained, as levelly as he could, that the sponsor was not Coca-Cola, but Royal Crown Cola. A slight deafness with which Ripley had become afflicted and a bad telephone connection had combined to lead Ripley off on the wrong Cola binge.

On this trip B. A. Rolfe persuaded Ripley to make a stage appearance with him in Kingston, Jamaica. B.A. had electric signs rigged up proclaiming "Ripley and Rolfe" before he even broached the plan to Rip. Then he told Bob that he couldn't back down after being advertised. It was an odd show, to put it mildly, with Ripley telling "Believe It or Nots" from the stage while Rolfe played *Roses of Picardy* on the cornet. Some thousand natives sat in profound silence through the show, and then burst into thunderous applause.

Ripley's reaction to his fame, and the manner in which he approached the task of sharing some of his fortune, was unpredictable at best. At times the fame seemed clearly to have gone to his head. He would treat employees almost as slaves, berating them, cursing them, summoning them to his presence merely to show visitors how they obeyed.

Depending on whom you asked, Ripley might be described as one of the most generous men who ever lived, or the most miserly. Dick Hyman went to work for Ripley in 1929, when Rip was just on the verge of his lush success. He employed Dick as a press agent at $60 a week and told him, "If I go up the ladder, so do you." Four years later when Dick quit, Ripley's income was better than $500,000; Hyman was still on the same old rung, getting $60 a week. He had just never been able to pin Ripley down on the subject of money.

Norbert Pearlroth, Ripley's chief researcher for more than twenty years, had some experiences with Ripley that were startling examples of generosity. Pearlroth used to make out his own salary check and then take it to Ripley for his signature. One day when he did this, Ripley looked at the check, became violently angry, tore the check into bits, stamped on the bits, and then declared in his outrage, "I *told* you I was giving you a raise!" He *hadn't* told Pearlroth, of course, but that wasn't important. On another occasion he called Pearlroth to inform him that he was going to give him a special bonus. Pearlroth sighed rather than waxing enthusiastic. Rip had told him the same thing the day before, in exactly the same language, the same inflections, and the same clearing of the throat. He had rehearsed his little speech to Pearlroth, and in his confusion or under the influence of liquor forgot he had delivered it.

Pearlroth also can recall the time he was trying to decide whether he could afford to send an adolescent daughter to an expensive private school; Ripley detected an appearance of worry and asked him what the trouble was. The next day

Pearlroth received from Ripley a check for $500, and on each of the following six days he received checks in the same amount. Ripley's reaction when Pearlroth thanked him for the $3500 was to say deprecatingly, "Next time ask me something *really* tough."

Ripley seemed to have a special quality of consideration for his discoverer, Carol Ennis. When he visited San Francisco or the Bay Area he always sent his chauffeur-driven limousine to pick her up and bring her to his hotel for lunch or dinner. When she visited New York in 1938 he put the car and a Russian driver at her disposal, and when she was leaving he brought her a gift.

"I wanted you to have something no other white woman could own," Ripley said as he gave her the little blue enamel disk on a gold chain. He explained that it was a Moslem device to ward off evil, and that the emblems were not supposed to pass outside a Moslem family. He wouldn't reveal how he had come by it, if he remembered at all.

Wherever he traveled, he managed to remember Bugs Baer's birthday, and invariably sent him elaborate birthday cards which he had drawn. The one for 1936, when Bugs hit the fifty-year mark, showed Bugs' head growing out of a long stem, and on it Rip had written, "Long Life! to the Half Century Plant." Rip had also arranged to have fifty of Bugs' friends in the newspaper, sports, and entertainment worlds sign beneath the cartoon.

During the years of World War II Ripley worked hard at the sort of thing overage celebrities were best fitted to do: help raise money and morale. He visited service hospitals, sold war bonds, and frequently opened Bion to servicemen going off to the wars or home on leave. He appeared on many special radio shows, including one "United States Treasury Hour" program that also included Fanny Brice, Miriam Hopkins, Deanna Durbin, John Charles Thomas, Arch Obeler, and Al Goodman's band. He did "Scramble," an NBC show designed to interest young men in flying. He was featured on a special radio series for the Co-ordinator of Inter-American Affairs, Nelson Rockefeller.

Ripley came up with hard-sell stories designed to promote the purchase of defense bonds. These stories were dramatized on radio and published in newspapers and magazines as public-service advertising. One told of "The Golden Hoard," a story with a morale that required an acrobatic application to make it fit the occasion. It concerned Ashurbanipal of Assyria, "the richest man who ever lived," worth a trillion and a half dollars (presumably computed at the then current exchange rate)—"75 times as much gold as is held by the United States treasury."

All this wealth, Ripley moralized, availed Ashurbanipal nothing. "Neither he nor his son had the sense to use this wealth for the good of their people or for their protection.

"And so it was comparatively easy for the Medes and the Persians to invade Assyria and enslave it. And finally, when it was too late—and defeat stared the great King in the face, Ashurbanipal, in terror, had a tremendous platform built of polished wood, in the city of Nineveh, and on top of this he heaped all of this wealth—142,000 tons of gold in 2,500,000 bricks (or ingots), each brick 28 inches in size and each brick valued at $50,000. This treasure formed a pyramid of shining gold nearly 100 feet high and," Ripley recounted with some special relish at this point, "in the intervening spaces he placed all of his jewels and personal belongings—his 478 wives on golden beds—his children—even his pet dog."

There was nothing left for old Ash at this point but to get himself "a great quantity of oil" from Mosul, pour it over the golden hoard and, after the torch had been applied, walk in and lie down among the burning billions. "And so the great Ashurbanipal, the richest man in the world, was consumed in his own wealth." That, too, was the end of the empire of the Assyrians.

"Why?" Ripley asked. "Because Ashurbanipal, who had practically all the money in the world, didn't do anything with it. So he and his country were lost."

Up to this point, a listener or reader might have assumed that Rip was preparing a petition to President Roosevelt to empty the vaults at Fort Knox, as the only means of saving the United States. He did manage, eventually, to bring his auditors to the lesson to be learned. On a crumbling wall in Nineveh, Rip pointed out, there still remains an inscription placed there at Ashurbanipal's direction, saying:

> *May God give you Ears to Hear and Eyes to See,*
> *And you will retain your Friends, your Wives,*
> *Your Pleasures and your Treasures.*

"Surely," Rip concluded with fervor, "we the people of America have 'Ears to Hear' and 'Eyes to See.' Surely we will not make the mistake made by Ashurbanipal.

"We *will* do something with *our money*. Enemies threaten us the same as they threatened Assyria in 7 B.C. [Rip meant the seventh *century*, B.C.] Obviously, there is only one thing to do: BUY DEFENSE BONDS and MAKE OUR MONEY DIRECTLY AVAILABLE TO OUR COUNTRY. Otherwise WE may become a melted, molten mass, and WE may be destroyed as Ashurbanipal was destroyed 2600 years ago.

"BELIEVE IT OR NOT!"

CHAPTER X

East Is East

AT the Oriental dinners he loved to give, Bob Ripley would always come up with a toast that represented the distilled wisdom of the East. One of his favorites was a prescription for long life attributed to Li Yung, who, by following it, was said to have lived two hundred and fifty years: "Walk like a pigeon, rest like a turtle, sleep like a dog, and always have contentment in your heart."

Increasingly but without success Rip sought that contentment in the wisdom and material things of the Orient. And for the exercise of this mood he acquired, in 1941, a new base of operations, a vast duplex apartment in Manhattan at Two West Sixty-seventh Street. Rip purchased this showplace, with most of the furnishings intact, from Burton Holmes, the world traveler and lecturer, and he filled in all the obvious and some unlikely crannies with items from his own storehouse of curiosa and *objets d'art*. This apartment became the scene of some epicurean triumphs and harrowing personal failures; even close friends were shocked at some of the things Ripley did; and to outsiders there often seemed to be a surrealistic quality to what went on.

The apartment, on the tenth floor, overlooked Central Park West and Sixty-seventh Street. The main living room, two stories high, faced the park. Rip's spacious bedroom was one story, facing the side street. Some of the lesser rooms faced on an interior court. The apartment consisted of ten rooms, many of which were never seen by his guests, such as the huge, dark, and outmoded kitchen.

The elevator at the tenth floor let its occupants out directly in the foyer of Ripley's apartment. To the left was Rip's bedroom—seemingly narrow, because of its great length—and the first impression of it was one of brooding darkness, accentuated by the heavy Spanish-Moorish polished wood, the ceiling, with its elaborately carved squares, the somber panels on the walls, and the thick, heavy, luxurious rugs, always a Ripley hallmark. On the wall were photographs of women, some merely friends, some rather more than that, all of them good-looking, all of them women he had liked or loved.

The living room, about fifty feet long, and duplex for the most part, commanded a superb view of Central Park, looking across it to Fifth Avenue. Bob loved to boast, "This is the only room in which you can see a beautiful sunset by looking *east*—believe it or not!" At certain times of the year, particularly late fall and early winter, the windows of the apartment houses on Fifth Avenue caught the reflection of the setting sun. Sometimes frosty clouds above the houses caught the pinkish afterglow of the sun to give an unreal effect to the whole scene. It looked like an idealized canvas.

"Pure Maxfield Parrish," breathed Louise Baer, the first time she witnessed this phenomenon.

At one end of the two-storied living room was a wide balcony, under which the room continued for another fifteen of its over-all fifty feet. When Bob held large dinner parties here —always with Chinese food, to maintain the harmony of the motif—he would set up a long table in the shape of a T, with the top of the T under the balcony. At a sit-down party, the room was large enough to entertain forty or more people comfortably.

Ripley always kept the room rather dimly lit, which lent shadowy mystery to the already exotic furnishings of the room. The whole apartment, in fact, was mistily illuminated, causing Bugs Bair to inquire if Rip had learned to draw in Braille.

At the far end of Rip's bedroom stood a partition wall that extended almost the width of the room. Behind this was a tiny alcove, dark and windowless, which probably had been designed as a small dressing room. Just fitting into it was a tiny, authentic Chinese marriage bed. It was covered with a brilliant red Chinese silk coverlet, and the hangings in the tiny alcove were of red and gold silk. It was Rip's great pleasure to extend the hospitality of this room to local Chinese friends on their wedding nights.

The contrast between the darkness of the master bedroom and the warm bright red glow of the alcove must have pleased Bob's artistic eye. To a Westerner, it was a bower of love, a concubine's nest, straight out of an Oriental harem. And if any of his guests chose to believe that was what it was, it was all right with Rip.

Nature had nothing on Ripley when it came to abhorring a vacuum. At Bion, everything was crowded—even some of the ceilings were carved and recessed into involved patterns. There are persons who cannot abide a conversational lull— Bob was that way about space. Everything had to be filled, and there was nothing austere in his quest for decorative effects. He liked the brightly colored, the intricately carved or intaglioed, the surprising or shocking. The minute, painstaking work of the Orient, particularly the Chinese, fascinated him, whether it was a mandarin coat with microscopic stitching or an ivory "bridge of life" carved with a multitude of figures no larger than a fair-sized ant.

The simplicity of the Greeks never appealed to Ripley.

There was no single item of antiquity or simple beauty in his entire collection. He had nothing simple and great from the early periods of China, such as a Tang horse. It wasn't that his collection wasn't both good and authentic, for it was, but many of his cherished possessions would have been bypassed by any serious art collector.

There was one outstanding virtue of Ripley's homes. Nowhere was there to be seen the regimented hand of the professional decorator. This was Rip, this was where he lived, these were things he'd acquired and cherished and made his own, and he put them where he damn well pleased. Few people could have lived among such decorations, but none who saw them ever forgot them, or, perhaps, escaped being haunted by them.

It was ironic that Ripley, who took such pride in his reputation as a collector of the unusual, should have had a great collection delivered to him intact. When he purchased the Central Park West home from Holmes, he also obtained that world traveler's considerable collection of Oriental art. All the truly fine, rare and exquisite articles in the duplex were part of the Holmes collection.

In the foyer of the apartment loomed a large gilded wooden statue, of a multi-armed Chinese Buddha, the god who gives and who takes away. It was set on a magnificently carved Chinese temple table of teakwood and gold lacquer which swarmed with writhing dragons. From the table's lower shelf a carved foo dog peered ferociously at the visitor. Behind this were two beautifully embroidered Chinese silk hangings.

Another item in the foyer not likely to be seen in a tour of Macy's basement was concealed in a closet, which Rip occasionally urged new acquaintances to open. Stark in a ceiling spotlight that blazed on automatically when the door was opened was a wooden statue of a man, so completely lifelike as to bring a gasp from the first-time viewer, a gasp which deepened when it was realized that the figure was completely nude. This was the aforementioned prime exhibit at Bion and the Odditoriums.

Inexplicably, Ripley in later years put a folded loincloth patch on the wooden man, who stood a few inches over five feet. What prompted Bob to this touch of modesty he never revealed. The shocker to his guests in opening the closet door was to find a man inside. That he was as naked as a jay bird was somewhat secondary.

The nonchalance with which he showed off the Buddha, and the keen delight he took in the wooden man, illuminated Rip's personality. With Rip, uniqueness beat artistic beauty ten ways from the jack.

A Japanese palanquin or sedan chair was in the living room. This was from the Holmes collection, and authentic. It must have been constructed for a young child, or perhaps a princess, for it was too small to hold a man, even Rip's Marching Chinese male friends. It was black and gold, with brass fittings and medallions, and completely enclosed, so that no one might see the occupant. It had little sliding panels as a door, and a tiny window with a reed screen. The bearers' pole was curved and of fine, heavy wood, carved and painted with little figures.

When a beautiful Oriental named Ming Jung was a guest at one of Rip's parties—and she was a guest at most of them— he would have her sit in it. She was tiny, and just fitted into it. The palanquin would then be closed, and, at a signal, Ming would slide the little window aside and her Oriental face would smile shyly at the guests. Bob liked this authentic touch.

Bob's parties were replete with authentic touches. Often he would preside in full mandarin costume. Almost invariably he would launch the affair with a toast, and he had a standard one for delivery at Chinese New Year's parties, with the hot rice wine.

"My illustrious ladies and gentlemen and friends. I am greatly honored by your illustrious presence in my humble home.

"This is the 4639th year of China, the first day of the first moon of the Horse Year, and I the humble son of the family of Rip Li do kowtow and bow three times to my ancestors that we are all gathered here in one big family.

"I am reminded of an honorable ancestor, Li Po, the poet, who liked his rice wine so well that he died seeking the reflection of the moon in the pool.

"My food, this night, may not be good, but I wish you to drink my wine.

"I hope you will eat a full belly—lose everything but become gloriously intoxicated.

"May the blessings of the gods be upon you and may clouds of incense burn your wishes to heaven!"

Sometimes Ripley would ask his old friend, Li Ling Ai, the distinguished and lovely Chinese lecturer and author, to conduct a running narrative describing each of the courses of the interminable Chinese dinner as it was served. Rip would pass a hundred-year-old egg around the table for inspection. Sometimes Li Ling Ai would find herself superseded by Ripley, who would take up the thread of the story and conduct the Oriental gastronomical tour on his own.

"This is shark's-fin soup," Ripley would explain, rudely breaking in on Li Ling's learned dissertation, "and it is shark's-fin soup as it is served in China, not what you get in some of the so-called Chinese restaurants around town. They serve American-Chinese food, which isn't the same thing at all."

Although Bob inveighed against New York's Chinese restaurants, he patronized some of them, particularly the smaller ones, which served authentic Chinese dishes. One spot he favored was Tung-Sai, down on Mulberry Street, in the shade of the New York State Building. It was operated by the late Shavey Lee, so-called Mayor of Chinatown, and is now run by his partner, Jim Yip Typond, a former lacrosse star at New York University.

"The larger Chinese restaurants," Ripley liked to pontificate, "serve food which Americans like to think is Chinese. The smaller ones serve the real thing. Did you ever see a Chinese as a customer in one of those big, brightly lit chow-mein places in midtown? Of course not. But Chinese eat out too. When you find where they eat, you've found the real thing."

Frequently, after such a discourse and while describing an item on his own menu, Ripley would look around the room, to make certain that his guests were listening to the course, not eating it, and add with a leer, "Among the Chinese, it's considered quite an aphrodisiac. I don't know whether this is so or not." While Ripley employed chopsticks quite adroitly, he was considerate in providing his guests with conventional tableware, lest they perish of malnutrition.

Chopsticks, and the inherent danger of finding a piece of sweet moist pork in one's lap, was not the only hazard lurking at Rip's parties. Just before the coffee, by which time he would have quaffed a good deal of rice wine, Rip would fill a rhinoceros horn with this potent beverage and, making a little speech about its significance as a loving cup, would drunkenly carry it around the table, sloshing it on the guests as he tried to pour it in their glasses.

Although Bob was voluble on the subject of Chinese cuisine, he was no trencherman. He cared very little about food, seemingly placing its value as a conversational item above its nutritional value, and he ate very little. He was a great nibbler, and his 'tween-meals snacks may well have dulled his appetite when the barrier was sprung at the dinner table.

When Ripley ate with small groups, the table setting often was more elaborate than the menu. In a billowing sea of gleaming napery and silverware, with ecru lace tablecloths, doilies, and napkins the size of bath towels, the main course was likely to be something as prosaic as roast lamb. And, at "family" luncheons, when Bob was supping with the staff, the provender was ordinarily hamburger. At the big dinner parties, however, the fare was both exotic and authentic.

When his guests' appetites had been satisfied, and Rip's supply of gastronomic information exhausted, he often would retire, leaving the party to wander among the collection of curios, which, as at Bion, ranged from chastity belts to medieval suits of armor and an occasional shrunken head thrown in. First-time guests were surprised by his sudden disappearance, and didn't realize that he was sparing them. For Rip had the somewhat startling habit of sucking his buck teeth after dinner, as though he were having the meal in two parts.

Rip in his fifties, during the 1940s, was not, his close friends would have to admit, always an altogether appetizing sight. The once-fine athlete was getting heavy, a development that tended to emphasize less attractive features. He was losing his hair, and he would let the few strands grow long, slick them back, and try to spread them around (Bugs Baer told a mutual friend about this time, "Rip's hair is so thin he starts combing it at the armpit"). With his round head, high cheekbones and seasonally swarthy complexion, Ripley jarringly called to mind a Japanese *suma* wrestler.

The deterioration was considerably more than skin deep. He became less careful about personal cleanliness, and his fingernails seemed always in need of attention. He had less and less control over his temper. He was more likely to be suspicious and arbitrary.

An acquaintance who was invited to the apartment for the first time in the mid-1940s recalls that Rip, for no particular reason, started complaining about his staff, about their lack of devotion to him and their general inadequacy. Actually they were trustworthy and talented people. Suddenly Ripley called out to three of them in another room—"screamed" would be a better word. All three responded and were told upon arrival, "I don't want ya. G'wan back." As they were leaving, but within earshot, Ripley turned to the acquaintance and said, "I just wanted to show ya' what I meant—just lackeys." It was a bone-chilling experience for the guest.

One of Rip's friends was a pretty German immigrant, who came to this country in the early thirties and applied for United States citizenship as soon as it was legally possible. By the time she was a full-fledged citizen, Adolf Hitler was storming over Europe like a thundercloud. The day she received her final papers, she carried them proudly to Ripley's West Sixty-seventh Street apartment, and was amazed to find a Nazi flag spread on the floor.

"Stomp on it!" ordered Ripley.

She thought it was a joke until she looked at her friend. The fire in his eyes was as fanatical as any that ever gleamed in Hitler's. She did as directed. The flag was a huge one (no one knew where Rip had obtained it), and the poor girl had to go up and down the living-room floor, performing this hoe-down of hate at Ripley's command. There were about twenty visitors to witness this mad scene, although it didn't seem to matter to Bob. He was past caring what people thought of him.

Bradley Kelly, the King Features Syndicate executive who

for many years guided Rip and his work, was making an informal little talk one day at a luncheon devoted to extravagant singing of Ripley's praises. To lend color to one point—the high standard of accuracy Rip maintained—Kelly recalled a slight mistake that had crept into the syndicated feature. Rip was furious, jumped to his feet, and exploded, "This just shows you what I'm up against at KFS!"

During this period Rip was propelled into deep-black moods by the death of friends. He could not abide even mention of the subject. And so even those closest to him did not know how hard he was hit when his beloved "Oakie," who had left a few years earlier to marry, died of cancer. It was not until a half-dozen years later, when he himself was near death, that Rip told Hazel Storer that "Oakie" was the only woman he had ever really loved.

Rip was sorely tried too by the failure of his younger brother, Douglas, to come up to expectations, and by the latter's heavy drinking. Those who would defend Doug pointed out that he had never had much big-brotherly counsel from Bob.

When Bob brought Doug east from Santa Rosa to live with him at Mamaroneck, Doug had no background for the mixed-up household in which he suddenly found himself. He was first confused, then bewildered, and finally hurt. Ripley was deeply disappointed that Doug didn't contribute more to the entourage. Perhaps he envisioned his younger brother as eventually pitching in on the management side and easing some of the burden he was carrying. There were the inevitable rows, for Ripley spared his brother no less than he spared his friends.

Joe Connolly used to make frequent visits to Bion, sometimes staying over. Joe didn't like the younger Ripley and was convinced he was merely one more headache to Rip, who was already carrying more than his quota. The blow-off came one night when Doug Ripley called Connolly, Rip's prime mentor, a free-loader and ordered him off the premises. It was something of a sensation, in a house where rows were the order of the day.

Later Rip got his brother a job at the "Believe It or Not" office in the *Daily Mirror* building, a minor assignment, but the younger Ripley handled it as if he were chief of staff. His gift for irritation so disrupted the staff that Connolly finally barred him from the building. Close as he was to Rip, Joe had to put his foot down to prevent chaos. Bob understood, and the expulsion of his younger brother put no strain on the ties of his friendship with Connolly.

Young Doug eventually married and settled in a house in Mamaroneck, complete with a Judas in the door. It was generally understood that Ripley had given this house to his brother, but when the will was read, it was learned that Bob had retained title to the house, and Doug had to purchase it from his brother's estate.

A climactic row between the brothers resulted in an estrangement which remained final until Bob's death. The blow-up came one morning in the apartment when Rip was on a ladder, rearranging some of his curiosities, and his young brother began heckling him.

Ripley descended the ladder, and the two had words. The words eventually led to action—or, at least, to threatening gestures—and Doug, making a sweeping motion with his arm, struck the ladder and sent it crashing to the stone floor, barely missing Bob's head. That did it.

"Out!" said Bob, pointing to the door like the father in *East Lynne*. It was the last word he ever spoke to his brother.

CHAPTER XI

Ripley at Sea

ASK an acquaintance of Bob Ripley for the artist's outstanding characteristic and the answer probably will be "buck teeth." Ask the same question of someone who was close to Ripley and the answer will be "his shyness." There is no doubt Ripley possessed both in profusion. He once had his teeth "rearranged," to use his own term—a strenuous, only partly successful straightening—but he never could do anything about his shyness.

The legend around Bion was that he had had his natural teeth extracted and replaced by pigs' teeth, which he claimed were impervious to cavities. One neighbor scotched this tale, however, by saying, "I don't believe it. Why would he have had the pigs' teeth put in bucked?"

Backward and ill at ease with people, particularly at first meeting, Rip was not shy where a dollar was concerned. He knew the value of publicity. Many of the full-dress parties Ripley threw at Bion or at his apartment were for the benefit of the advertising agencies or his radio sponsors. He always was lavish at parties for press and magazines. He was a natural host, in that he wanted all his guests to enjoy themselves, and once the party was under way, Rip neither knew nor cared whether it was for business or for pleasure.

Rip was not comfortable even with fellow workers in the King Features vineyard. One night at the Hotel Pierre, at the annual KFS dinner party and dance, he was dismayed to hear the M.C., Ralph Edwards, burble, "Now we're going to play Truth or Consequences, and our first two contestants will be two Bobs—Bob Ripley and Bob Considine."

We got up from the same table and advanced warily on the brightly lighted dance floor. After each of us had failed to solve an unsolvable riddle, we were told that the "consequences" were that we must each pick up a suitcase filled with women's clothing and underclothing, race across the breadth of the dance floor, open the suitcases, select and put on a single one of the garments or armor enclosed, close the suitcases, and race across to the opposite "base."

"On your mark, get set, go!" thundered the excessively enthusiastic man.

We started off together, but only one of us made it. And that one wasn't Rip. He made a screeching U turn on the floor, headed out through the tables, dropped the suitcase, and was gone—beet-red and enraged. Louis Alwell, of INS, picked up the fallen suitcase and went through with the preposterous game. Ripley had to be begged thereafter to attend a KFS social function.

Ripley was a different man aboard his Chinese junk *Mon Lei*, which he bought in 1946. It pleased Ripley because it was outlandish, and it also was an effective form of advertising for the Ripley enterprises. He loved to travel on the junk, finding it both stimulating and relaxing. Frequently he made business trips on it, taking one to Boston during which what must have been the entire Chinese population of that city turned out to welcome him. It wasn't exactly a coincidence that Ripley was opening a radio contest over six New England stations that same week.

Joe Willicombe, publicist for King Features as well as a close friend, arranged one such junket on the junk for Hart-

ford, Connecticut. Ripley was to be the guest of honor at a
large dinner party given by the Hartford *Times*. The plan
called for *Mon Lei* to sail from Bion up Long Island Sound
to Old Saybrook, Connecticut, and then up the Connecticut
River to Hartford.

Willicombe, better than a green hand in the public-rela-
tions dodge, arranged a big "do." The publisher and editor of
the *Times* and General Jonathan Wainwright and other no-
tables were waiting dockside to give Ripley a rousing welcome.

All the dignitaries were assembled, peering down river for
Mon Lei but finding no sign of her sails. Willicombe, calculat-
ing all the things that could happen, finally decided to make
a personal check. He phoned Bion, learned the time of departure, and realized that the junk was at least an hour over-
due. Then he jumped into his car and started down the shore-
line of the river, looking for any traces of the *Mon Lei*.

At Middletown, Connecticut, about twenty miles down
river, he found *Mon Lei* contentedly tied up to a dock, the
junk's roving captain taking his ease on the deck.

"What the hell are you doing tied up in Middletown?"
Willicombe yelled.

"This ain't Middletown, this is Hartford," replied the captain evenly.

Willicombe told the captain that this most certainly wasn't
Hartford, but the only response he could get was, "Mr. Ripley
says this is Hartford and that's good enough for me!"

Going below, Joe found Bob relaxing in one of the cabins.
A long argument ensued, with Ripley insisting that the craft
was docked at Hartford. Finally Willicombe coaxed Ripley
into his car and took off for the Hartford Towers, where the
dinner was being held.

It was inevitable that the rival paper should hear of the

snafu involving the *Times'* guest of honor, and the next day a
banner line on page three read: "RIPLEY ERRS, MISTAKES MID-
DLETOWN FOR HARTFORD." Naturally, a goof-off of such proportions by a globe-trotter of Ripley's reputation formed the
foundation for a humorous story, but not one which publicist
Willicombe cared to paste in his scrapbook.

Mon Lei wasn't exactly the *Queen Mary* for arriving on
time. In August 1947 the junk, and Rip, were due in Albany,
New York for a big wingding staged by the *Times-Union*,
which carried his cartoon. Doug Storer, Ken McGregor, an
NBC representative, and George Lefferts, who wrote the
program, arrived the night before to get everything prepared
for the welcome, including alerting the fire department to let
go with its sirens.

Crowds thronged the Dunn Memorial Bridge, where *Mon
Lei* was scheduled to dock. The leading lights of the city, a
flotilla of yachts, and a contingent of Sea Scouts were on hand
—but no *Mon Lei*.

Once again, Willicombe had to search for the wayward
mariner. He found *Mon Lei,* well south in the Hudson, completely helpless and disabled. He phoned Storer, who was
able to cajole a Navy LSVT to go down river and tow in the
junk.

Mon Lei merits a full description. Built of hand-hewn teak
and camphor wood, *Mon Lei* was fifty feet long, with a seven-
teen-foot beam, and drew six and one-half feet of water. It
was a genuine "Foochow Fisher" junk, such as was used on
the Foochow River. Flatbottomed, it had a shoal draft and
no keel. Its bow didn't split the water but, rather, glided over
it. The flat bottom is a necessity on boats of this type because
of the numerous sand bars encountered on voyages between
Foochow, Shanghai, and the lower Yangtze ports.

Mon Lei's foremast projected, jiblike, over the bow, and the massive mainmast was amidships. The light mizzen, high on the poop deck, was set off-center for convenience in stays, going about from one tack to another.

On *Mon Lei*, Ripley was able to combine his passion for authenticity and his affection for things Chinese. It was painted in the original colors of all the Foochow fishing boats, a mixture of red, blue, white, and assorted other hues. The decoration of a junk varies according to its home port, each particular river and seaport having its own colors. Any Chinese sailor can tell at once by observing the colors of a junk which port she sails from.

The meaning of the word "junk" is vague, stemming from the Portuguese "*junco*" and the Javanese "*jon*," but is mainly an Occidental corruption of a South China word, "*le planks*," indicating the size or width of the boat. *Mon Lei* is the equivalent of "*Bon Voyage*." Literally, it means "Ten Thousand" or "Infinity." The Great Wall of China also was called "*Mon Lei*."

The history of *Mon Lei* fascinated Ripley as much as did the craft itself. It was built for the private comfort of a Chinese war lord in 1939 by the Wo Hop Company of Hong Kong. When the Japanese captured Hong Kong, the war lord beat it, and the invaders confiscated his craft. As the fortunes of war began to turn, three Chinese and an American managed to bribe their way into possession of the boat and begin the perilous crossing of the Pacific to the United States. It took them eighty-six days to reach San Francisco.

Ripley eventually came across the boat in a Baltimore shipyard, bought her for $7500, and began the massive job of reconditioning and decorating her. Bob installed powerful diesel engines that enabled the boat to cruise at a clip which would have startled her Wo Hop builders.

Never was so ancient a vessel so thoroughly and completely

modernized. Despite the power in her hold, it suited Rip to have the (purposely) patched sail up at all times, which acted as a drag on the junk when it was running under power. Boatmen in the Long Island Sound at first rubbed their eyes but eventually grew accustomed to the strange sight of the junk proceeding toward the Atlantic with its sails billowing toward the Pacific. It rode high out of the water, with little or no keel and a tallish poop deck aft.

Showers, hot and cold running water, Beautyrest mattresses, and a ship-to-shore radio-telephone were some of the conveniences Ripley installed, so that the craft became a bewildering amalgamation of the sixteenth and twentieth centuries. It was, no matter how you looked at it, an odd ship. But it matched its host and most of its guests perfectly.

Ripley couldn't have chosen a more appropriate spot aboard *Mon Lei* to hang the work of a long-dead artist. The painting was hung in the junk's "head." The artist must have been an Oriental Chic Sale. The activity of the woman portrayed was lost on most of the visitors, unless they inspected it most closely or were familiar with Chinese plumbing.

Because of an ancient Chinese belief that a boat moves only because there is a dragon inside of it, Rip took paints and brushes to the engine room and transformed the diesels into the likeness of traditional Chinese dragons. *Mon Lei* may still carry the only diesels on the seven seas possessing eyes, teeth, and whiskers.

Ripley put quite a bit of his Oriental collection into *Mon Lei*—paintings, carvings, and the like, as well as heavy teak furniture. Bob also caused considerable exterior decorating to be done. The elliptical transom stern of a junk always has afforded the artistic Chinese an opportunity to display his fantastic originality of design and color. Rip overlooked no bets along this line.

The wheelhouse was decorated with famous Chinese say-ings—in Chinese characters, of course. The quotation on the bow side meant, "May she sail like a flying dragon and move like a leaping elephant." She often did.

The characters on the portside of the wheelhouse read, "Fast time, long voyage," and those on the starboard stood for "One way peace" and "Long wind, ten thousand miles." On the aft end of the wheelhouse, another Chinese saying read, "Straight wind, straight water."

Ripley was meticulous in following all the ancient tradi-tions of the Chinese sailors in his decorations, such as having the butterfly of good luck painted on the bow. On the owner's flag Bob chose the Yin and Yang symbol, since it is the old-est symbol of the Chinese. Yang signifies heaven, sun, and light; Yin stands for earth, moon, and darkness. Yang is the superior and male principle of nature, and Yin is the inferior and female principle of nature. *Mon Lei* had only one Yang, but many Yins.

Eyes were painted on each side of the bow of the junk, because Rip insisted this was in keeping with another Chinese tradition: "No got eyes, no can see, no can see, no can walk." He was vague about the dynasty which produced this.

There were other Chinese symbols aboard *Mon Lei*, not all of which had to do with navigational blessings. Samuel F. Pryor, vice-president of Pan American Airways and a friend of Ripley's ever since they shared a room together at the Pittsburgh Athletic Club during a housing shortage induced by the 1925 World Series, recalled one of his last visits with the cartoonist.

"Rip sailed the Chinese junk into Greenwich harbor, with a little Chinese girl friend on board," recalled Pryor. "Bob went off to play golf—I believe with Lowell Thomas—and I took my mother and another dowager from Greenwich down to visit the junk."

The dowagers were shown around the junk by Ripley's little Chinese friend, Sam tagging along after them. They innocently asked the meaning of the large symbol over the bed in the master stateroom. Without changing her expression, the Chinese girl told the ladies it was the highest compliment one Chinese could pay to another.

"And that is?" asked one of the ladies.

"It means," said the girl, as demurely as if she were reciting the multiplication table, "I wish you one thousand lays."

"Ah yes, how interesting," chorused the women, thinking of Hawaiian wreaths.

Ripley had bells on the four corners of the pagoda pilothouse as a musical call to the gods and observed the tradition of having a gong sound each time *Mon Lei* sailed to ward off evil spirits. For reasons known only to himself, Rip also had aboard a deadly impaling instrument and an execution sword that he used to say was the longest in the world.

Enthroned in the cabin of *Mon Lei* was Ho Tai, the jolly god of happiness, who makes one's wish come true if one but rubs the god's stomach. Ripley also had a gaily colored beaded prayer wheel, which supposedly said one thousand prayers at each turn of the wheel, and a blue pillow embroidered with the "forbidden stitch." (The "forbidden stitch," Bob liked to inform his visitors, was a stitch so fine, the maidens of China went blind executing it until an empress forbade the use of it.)

One feature of *Mon Lei*, suggested not by Chinese tradition but by the irrepressible Bugs Baer, was square portholes.

"In case any Swedes come aboard and want to look out a window," Bugs explained to puzzled passengers.

Also on the junk was a statue of the many-armed Buddha of Benevolence, ready to bestow multitudinous blessings from his many hands. As a final touch of elegance—and one only Ripley and no mere Chinese war lord could have thought of —was gold-plated anchor and red ropes woven of nylon.

Ripley had special stationery made up for *Mon Lei*, embossed with an excellent painting of the junk executed by Bob himself. It was a miniature of a superior cover Rip had done for *Motor Boating* magazine.

Ripley's great personal attachment for the junk was touching. It not only gratified his deep desire to ride his Chinese hobby but it represented to him a security he couldn't be sure of in any of his three residences on land. When Bob was afloat in *Mon Lei*, even if only on the sound a few miles offshore from Bion, it meant that his privacy couldn't be invaded. The people aboard were those he had personally selected and could surely dominate.

Personal privacy always was a big issue with Ripley, one of the stranger quirks of a man who was host to so many outsize parties. His shyness gave him an instinctive distrust of strangers, although it afforded no protection at all against the moochers and sycophants who continually latched onto him. He was a soft touch for any hard-luck story, even when he was fairly certain that the story was an invention. But he could be as unmoved as a cornerstone too, if that was his mood.

Ripley's fondness for *Mon Lei* extended even to the extent of making use of her when she was tied up at the dock at Bion. He repeatedly found excuses to hold small luncheon parties on the junk. Sometimes he would discover he had invited more than could be comfortably fed aboard the junk, in which case a buffet luncheon would be set up in the dining room of the house, eaten from tables on the terrace.

Almost invariably these luncheons ended with Rip and his guests swarming aboard *Mon Lei* for a trip around the sound.

Ripley delighted in telling visitors of the many features of modern shipbuilding which have been adapted from the Chinese junk. He usually led off the lecture by stating that the Chinese had invented and were using the compass as early as A.D. 1112, long before it was known in the Western world. This was disputable, but, true or not, had nothing to do with *Mon Lei*. Rip also would point out that Chinese shipbuilders were the first to employ watertight compartments and that the junk was the first sailing ship with individual cabins—or staterooms, as they later came to be called.

For a man who possessed the zest for travel that Ripley had, the junk, plowing along at somewhat less than the speed of sound, was far from the ideal mode of transportation, but Bob seemed to find more peace aboard *Mon Lei* than anywhere else. Even when he had grown unusually quick-tempered, a sail on the junk relaxed him.

Ripley took the junk to most of the ports of call along Long Island Sound and, as related, sailed it to Albany and Boston on occasion. Using the Inland Waterway, Bob also cruised from New York to Palm Beach on *Mon Lei*. At Palm Beach he had a special dock built for the junk on Lake Worth.

After Ripley's sudden death, when his advisers could find no will (one turned up later), *Mon Lei* was thoroughly searched. Some of Rip's friends, knowing of his devotion to the craft, believed he might have hidden the will on the boat for sentimental reasons.

Frequently Rip reverted to Chinese costumes when sailing *Mon Lei*, and he saw to it that these costumes were as authentic as the junk itself. Rip, on the poop deck in full regalia, complete from slippers to hat, could have passed for the original war lord who owned the potbellied vessel.

Worn only on more or less formal occasions was a regulation captain's outfit: double-breasted blue flannel coat with brass buttons, white cap with gold braid and gleaming patent-leather visor. Rip wore white flannel trousers with this but sometimes lent a jarring note by easing his feet in slippers or sandals.

It was on one idle Sunday's cruise aboard *Mon Lei* that Ripley dropped a remark treasured by his friends for years. It was a balmy summer day, and Rip decided that his full mandarin costume would be just the thing.

The sight of *Mon Lei*'s sails, inscribed, expletive-like, with Chinese characters, attracted its usual attention from other boats, and one, a small cabin cruiser, came close to get a look at *Mon Lei* and her occupants. This was nothing new for Rip's friends, for they were used to the junk's arousing curiosity, but it was the eyes of his guests which that day bugged when the cruiser came closer. Its occupants were a middle-aged couple who were either practicing nudists or devoted to total sun-bathing.

"Look, Rip!" shouted one of his guests.

Ripley, engaged in concocting a drink which had as many ingredients as boardinghouse hash, turned a disdainful glance at the uncovered pair.

"Exhibitionists!" he snorted contemptuously. No matter in how bizarre a fashion Rip behaved, he considered he was doing only what came naturally. Everybody was a bit wacky but Bob.

He began to spend as much of his free time as possible aboard, possibly seeing in it a compensation for the decline of his globe-trotting. He may have felt that when he was aboard *Mon Lei,* he was back again in his beloved China, a China closed to him forever when the iron fist of Mao Tse-tung slammed down.

The purchase of the junk emphasized the ability of Ripley to combine business and pleasure. *Mon Lei* was symbolic of

China and the Orient and typified Bob's affection for the exotic. No one else in America, indeed in the Western Hemisphere, owned a junk, which in itself was a great advertisement for Bob and his "Believe It or Not" promotions. It was what his public expected from a man who challenged their credulity every morning over their breakfast cups.

While the purchase and conversion of *Mon Lei* was expensive, it was cheaper than buying a yacht. The junk was navigable and comfortable, luxuriously so. Besides, lots of people owned yachts. Ripley would have been bored stiff on one.

Joe Willicombe regarded the junk as something of a mixed blessing. It made his task of publicizing Ripley easier, but it was his albatross too.

After Ripley concluded that only gin laced with grapefruit juice was fit for a man to stomach, no one had any idea where he might wind up in the junk. So Willicombe called for an ally—the United States Coast Guard.

On one occasion Joe arrived in Boston a day early to set the stage with newspapers, TV, and radio for the Ripley visitation. The procedure was routine: arrange for the keys to the city, get out the Boy Scout Bugle and Drum Corps, line up a parade, a cocktail reception, and dinner.

Ripley was due at four in the afternoon. Everything was set. Four o'clock arrived, but no sign of the mariner or his offbeat craft. Fortunately a Coast Guard cutter was tied up at the pier where Rip was due. In it Joe immediately put to sea. The junk was spotted fourteen miles out, headed in the general direction of Europe.

As the cutter closed in, Joe studied Ripley through binoculars. The most worried look Joe had ever seen on Rip's face split into a wide grin. Obviously he was glad to see the cutter. But when the skipper of the cutter asked him why he was headed out to sea, Bob icily denied that he was. Actually he and his odd crew had been completely lost.

"I knew where I was every second," he said gruffly to the helpful Coast Guardsman.

Not all of Willicombe's problems with Ripley and *Mon Lei* stemmed from the fact that America's most publicized globe-trotter had no bump of direction. The junk once visited Washington, where "Believe It or Not" had long been a top feature in the *Times-Herald*. One of the editors, an engaging fellow, decided that somewhere along the line he should drop in at Ripley's suite at the Mayflower and pay him a courtesy call.

The editor arrived for cocktails, accompanied by his newest and prettiest girl friend. Willicombe ushered them into the suite and called out to Rip in the next room, where he was dressing, to alert him that his guests had arrived. Out popped Rip immediately, attired in nothing but a red bathrobe decorated with dragons. The robe scarcely covered a legal amount of bulging epidermis. He shook hands in his court-liest style and retreated to his dressing room.

One look at the editor's face was enough to let Joe know he was faced with a diplomatic crisis. The editor nodded to draw Joe aside, and in low but heated tones asked where in the hell this fellow Ripley got his nerve to receive him and his girl friend practically nude.

The *Times-Herald* was one of King Features Syndicate's best-paying outlets. Joe explained that in the Orient, where Ripley had spent so much time, the great Chinese potentates always received their favored guests in just such regalia. "That was a ceremonial robe," Joe went on wildly, "and Rip thought he was doing you and the young lady a great honor by receiving you in this fashion."

This hastily contrived gamesmanship mollified the editor.

"Isn't that nice," he observed. "Good old Ripley! He thinks of everything, doesn't he?"

Ripley's inability to swim a stroke somewhat complicated things for this increasingly ancient mariner. He simply never learned and never cared, something of a contradiction for one who lived at the New York Athletic Club as a young man, a club which had several of the nation's best swimmers and water-polo teams.

"I think I attended every swimming dinner held at the club during the twenty years I lived there," Bob boasted, "and never went into the pool once."

This, to Rip, constituted a sort of personal "Believe It or Not," and he gilded the lily further with his explanation of it. "There was no such thing as 'the ole swimmin' hole' around where I lived in Santa Rosa, and I never had enough money to go all the way to the beach. My father, though, was a good swimmer. When he ran away from his home in West Virginia at the age of fourteen, he swam the Ohio River on his way to California."

The fact that he couldn't swim failed to keep Rip from dressing for a dip from time to time. The Ripley swimming costume had to be seen to be believed, and even then was as incredible as some of his newspaper items. He wore droopy trunks that reached to his knees, a fashion which went out shortly after World War I. Sometimes he wore a sports shirt for a top piece; more often than not, his tattered old bathrobe. Conceivably he was the only man in America who wore a pith helmet with swimming trunks.

That he couldn't swim never bothered Bob when he was aboard *Mon Lei,* even at its rollingest. He once had a party aboard the junk on Lake Okeechobee in Florida, when a considerable enough storm arose so that all boats were ordered to take shelter. Ripley told the captain to disregard the orders and keep going. "We're so far out now," he said, "that it's just as easy to go all the way across as it is to return." No one dared dispute such logic.

As it turned out, it wasn't easy at all. The series of black squalls, with howling winds punctuated with vivid flashes of lightning, into which the junk wallowed gave the tub and its people a harrowing time before reaching port.

Whether Bob was courageous or just headstrong was a frequent subject of debate among his friends.

At Palm Beach he once arranged a sail for his friends and neighbors on Lake Worth. He loaded the junk with guests, many of whom maintained winter places at Palm Beach. The cruise, although scheduled to be short, was to be de luxe. In addition to his guests, Rip put his servants aboard and enough provisions, including spirits, to reach Pitcairn Island. He passed out Chinese hats from his treasured collection to the guests, to serve as sunshades.

It was a successful party, and the success apparently went to Rip's head. Awash with gin and grapefruit juice, and exuberant with the feel of the deck under his feet and the sound and fury of a party going full blast, Rip commanded the captain to head out through the inlet to the Atlantic Ocean.

It was a gusty day. Even normally placid Lake Worth had wreaths of whitecaps. At the inlet, the water boiled like a millrace, stirred by the high winds and a fast-rising tide. The skipper, Captain Platt, took one look and informed the owner that the little junk wouldn't be able to take it.

Ripley by this time had a full head of steam, even if *Mon Lei* didn't.

"She sailed across the Pacific, didn't she?" he demanded.

Several of Ripley's guests, who had boats of their own and knew the inlet, didn't believe Bob actually meant to have the captain take the junk out to sea. He did, however, and when the captain reluctantly headed into the open waters of the Atlantic, there was a concerted roar of protest.

Instead of accepting the protest as evidence of the risk he was running, Ripley took it as a disparagement of *Mon Lei*. He went about assuring everybody that there was nothing to worry about, but once in the open sea, *Mon Lei* decided the issue herself. As soon as the junk's pug-nosed prow hit the white water she began giving a demonstration of the *Hesperus* in her last throes.

The helmsman had no control of *Mon Lei* as she slithered about. After a senselessly long time, Ripley yielded to the clamor of his nautically hep guests and the junk put back into the quieter waters of Lake Worth.

Despite the fact that he had frightened and offended his guests, and nearly foundered the junk—which would have put him, as a nonswimmer, in a profound predicament—Ripley considered the junket a huge success. His only complaint was that his guests didn't return the Chinese hats he had given them as protection against the sun.

"They thought they were souvenirs, the dopes," he said bitterly.

Ripley took the junk to Florida in 1947, before he bought his home at Palm Beach. Actually, he bought the Hi-Mount house for the junk. *Mon Lei* could operate all year in Florida's balmy climate, and Bob, after buying Hi-Mount, spoke seriously of establishing it as his permanent residence—insofar as he could have a permanent residence anywhere—and conducting all his operations from there: cartoons, radio, and television, into which form of art he was just thrusting a tentative foot.

When Ripley did purchase Hi-Mount in late 1947 he had

a special, pagoda-like dock built for *Mon Lei* at the foot of his expansive lawn, which ran to the edge of Lake Worth.

The junk he loved so dearly betrayed him, in a sense. It brought to light one of Ripley's frailties that only his most intimate friends knew about. He was one of the most resonant snorers of all time. Those who were his house guests in the spacious homes he maintained at Bion, Central Park West, and Hi-Mount weren't exposed to his clarion nocturnal serenades, but in the close quarters of *Mon Lei* on overnight jaunts there was no getting away from it. Ripley, in repose, was a sawmill working double shifts.

Sleeping quarters on the *Mon Lei* were as compact as a glove. On one trip, Hazel Storer had to share the master's bedroom with Rip and a secretary, while Doug and the captain slept in the other bedroom. The mate slept in the wheelhouse. Han, the Chinese cook, had a compartment that looked like "solitary" on Captain Bligh's *Bounty*—a tiny purchase under a hatch up forward. There was just room in it for an extremely small berth and for Han, once in, to remove his trousers. The cook lowered himself into this cubicle from the deck. On the hatch cover, Rip, in a burst of well-researched sentiment, had painted a Chinese character meaning roughly "The House of Han."

There were those who felt sorry for the cook when they peered into his dim, cramped quarters. Others, who had had the experience of overnight trips with Rip, envied the chopper of suey.

"Don't feel sorry for Han," advised one. "He's got something nobody else on *Mon Lei* has—privacy. And, what's more, he's the only one who can't hear Ripley snore."

The voyages of *Mon Lei* were never without incident and were sometimes unnerving even for Rip. Once, under the pressure of a business commitment, he flew to Palm Beach instead of embarking on the long-planned trip there from Bion aboard the *Mon Lei* via the Inland Waterway. He assigned two of his most treasured female guests to make the trip, to check on the two-man crew and otherwise act as his representatives. En route, the girls fell in love with the crew and vice versa. So they were married.

"Why didn't you fire them?" a friend asked Ripley, when he described the arrival of the strangest honeymoon barge in the annals of matrimony.

"I thought of it," Rip acknowledged. "But I liked all of them too much. Besides, it simplified the matter of sleeping quarters aboard the junk."

CHAPTER XII

Few Happy Days

THE happiest days of Rip's late years were probably spent at his Palm Beach home, after he took possession in February 1948.

Rip was so anxious to get settled at Hi-Mount that he beat the moving vans to the door. On the day he took over, only one van had arrived out of the caravan that was rolling southward from Bion. These vans contained everything that Rip felt he needed to turn a house into a homelike museum.

The van that arrived that first day contained, along with some furniture, a large collection of Chinese pottery, a concert grand piano, and an Oriental rug that seemed, from its size, to have been a special order for the foyer of the Radio City Music Hall. But the van contained nothing so useful as pots and pans, linen, or a bed. Nor did it contain Han and Billy, Rip's Chinese servants, who were riding down on one of the vans which had been delayed in South Carolina.

That first night, therefore, Rip and the little lady who accompanied him had to "rough it" on the Florida gold coast, curled up on cot and sofa and unattended by the soft-shod Orientals upon whom Bob was so dependent for his creature comforts. Doug and Hazel Storer were there too, but prudently decided to stay at a hotel on the beach.

Rip was happy as a nesting bird that day, giving wildly conflicting directions about the furniture arrangement, pushing the grand piano around constantly, and laying the vast rug in the even vaster living room.

Among the contents of that first van was an object of art-lessness that the Storers had never seen before—a round, battered, cheap wooden table.

"Watch that table!" Ripley sang out to the van men, as if supervising the moving of the Venus de Milo to a new wing in the Louvre.

The Storers wondered why, aloud. They had known him intimately now for fifteen years, had virtually lived with him, and had never seen this object of his tenderness.

"It's my good-luck piece," Ripley said, as if talking to strangers. "I'm never without it. On this table I drew my first cartoons."

At the end of the long day of unloading and arranging the mismatched contents of Van Number One, Ripley suggested that all hands were too tired to go to a restaurant.

"We'll dine here," he said.

An inspection of the barracks-sized kitchen showed only an abandoned coffeepot. So Storer went off into the night and soon returned with mounds of cold cuts, baked beans, and paper containers of Michelob beer. It was Rip's favorite malt brew, and his eyes lit up at sight of Storer's happy surprise.

Before a blazing fire which Storer built on the big stone hearth, Ripley, who doted on splendor, as he knew splendor, ate with relish the simple food spread out on the battered old table.

The Storers, who knew a dozen of his moods, never remembered his being more relaxed, happier, or more gay. He had found contentment in a shambles, this wholly unpredictable man. They pondered the amazing change, and concluded that it must be that—for once—Ripley was not under the pressure of being a host of whom the wildest follies were expected.

In time, Hi-Mount acquired the cluttered décor that was its owner's hallmark. Upon Ripley's death, eighteen months after taking possession, the estate appeared to have been stocked by offbeat collectors over a period of years. But it was a one-man job. Rip didn't need much time to turn a place into a museum, one with Odditorium overtones.

The jaded colony of Palm Beach adopted Ripley. The toniest of entrenched dowagers and their brittle escorts sought invitations to his casually flamboyant soirees, either at his home or aboard the junk. To gain Rip's favor they plied him with invitations to their own endless cocktail and swimming parties. In another period, Ripley would have leaped at such offers, but not now. By 1948 Bob had forgotten how to be a guest. He had played host to too many thousands, tens of thousands. He had directed and ridden herd on too many feasts, too many bacchanals. He could not be bothered with the formality of ordering another drink. At home, all he had to do was hold out his hand and Han would place one in it. It pleased him to turn down invitations by the score, and to limit his own guests at Hi-Mount to a few friends that he felt understood him.

The place was a new toy, and he never ceased to marvel over its pool, gardens, dock, and a cluster of solar reflectors which produced hot water.

"It works!" he would exclaim to visitors as he showed off this particular wonder. His voice packed the same awe that Sam Goldwyn's had, when the famed producer first saw a sundial and gasped, "What'll they think of next?"

Ripley would have drowned even in the shallow end of his pool, yet he resented it if guests—even those who either couldn't swim or didn't want to—turned down his insistent invitations to take a dip. One morning, upon leaving his bed and waddling to a window to survey his domain, he detected

Hazel Storer splashing through a pre-breakfast swim. Ripley pulled on a robe, went down to the Chinese-pottery-lined side of the pool, and warmly thanked her.

It was not a sufficient excuse for a guest to say, upon being invited to use the pool, "No, thanks. I just had a dip in the ocean." Rip and the Atlantic Ocean were on the outs.

"What's the ocean got that my pool hasn't, outside of waves?" he demanded of a suddenly frightened guest one afternoon.

After a bit, the guest came up with what should have been a crushing reply. "Salt water," he said.

Ripley leaped up triumphantly.

"Hah!" he said. "I've had my pool re-engineered so that I can fill it with either fresh or salt water. Now, which do you prefer?"

The fellow went for a swim.

He became more selective about the people around him. Though hardly a man with a marked sense of humor, Rip preferred friends with agile minds. He soon found them at Palm Beach: Walter Shirley, a former song-plugger for Irving Berlin and soon to become one of the most successful men in real-estate development; the irrepressible Rube Goldberg; Bugs; and two lively old New Yorkers who were fixtures on the Palm Beach scene during "the season"—Joe Bannon and Doc Kelton. Bannon, once a hard-bitten circulation manager for Hearst (only the hard-bitten survived in Bannon's prime), had retired to devote himself to clipping his coupons. It was said of Kelton, his constant companion, that Doc retired at the age of sixteen.

The two of them made Rip's house ring with the laughter of many a hearty tale, laughter that at times almost drowned out the sound of Bannon mixing a cocktail of his own dark invention, christened "The Royal Blood of Ireland."

Joe could always break Rip up with a booming story of how Bannon's pastor thwarted thieving collection-basket passers by requiring them to carry a cockroach in the free hand and return it, alive, at the end of the collection. Bob would writhe with laughter, then go through the house or out on the sweeping lawn to gather up a guest or two and have Bannon repeat the tale.

Bannon and Kelton returned Ripley's affection, but not to the extent of spending a night at Hi-Mount. They would always find ways and means of getting back to their suite, usually at the Breakers, or to some beach-front mansion Bannon had rented.

"I like Rip, he's swell," Bannon would explain, "but I'd just as soon spend a night in the old Eden Musée as stay at that joint. It'd give a fellow the shakes."

Those among the regulars of Florida's Gold Coast who made it to Ripley's for any of his larger parties often found the scene bewildering. One afternoon a stately dowager, threading her way through what might have been a garden scene from *The World of Suzie Wong*, spotted Bannon. She had a question to ask.

"Mr. Bannon," she inquired, pointing with her lorgnette, "just who is that exquisite Oriental-type young woman over there, and who is her escort?"

"Lady," Joe said, lapsing into his lower-Manhattan accent, "you can't tell the guests without a scorecard."

Ripley had a consuming affection for animals, far beyond what he showed in his personal relationships with people. Here his favorite Cyclops has been hoked up to match his name. UNITED PRESS INTERNATIONAL PHOTO

As a young man, Ripley was of major-league caliber. New York Giants' Manager John McGraw spoke seriously to Rip of a career in professional baseball. UNITED PRESS INTERNATIONAL PHOTO

Ripley, on his last trip to the Orient, in 1948, pauses in the Hawaiian Islands to supervise a "Truth or Consequences" penalty—a "permanent wave" from the beach at Waikiki.

On Hollywood Road, in Hong Kong, Ripley fulfills a "Consequence." He gets fifty Chinese to sign a scroll stating that "Leo Durocher is the greatest manager in baseball." However, he could not get them to chant "Yippee, yippee, yippee for Lippee, Lippee, Lippee," as planned.

In the Philippines, Ripley takes the measure of a boa constrictor. To bring back a boa was another "Truth or Consequences" penalty.

Ripley and the famous lifelike self-statue of the Japanese artist, Masakichi, true down to the very last detail.

WIDE WORLD PHOTO

Ripley joins a songfest. The singers are, left to right: Arthur "Bugs" Baer, Walter Shirley, Bob Considine, former New York Mayor William O'Dwyer, and Ripley, who couldn't sing a note but always liked to try.

Ripley's last big party. In December of 1948, King Features gave a costume party at Toots Shor's restaurant, in New York, to celebrate the thirtieth anniversary of the "Believe It or Not" cartoon feature. Some of the celebrators were, left to right: Bugs Baer, cartoonist Ham Fisher, editor Harold Kern, Ripley, and Toots Shor.

UNITED PRESS INTERNATIONAL PHOTO

CHAPTER XIII

Last Voyage

DURING the early days at Hi-Mount Ripley's mood was somewhat lighter than usual. Together with the simple enjoyment of a new possession were plans for another trip to his beloved China. The spark for the journey had flared at a Christmas party a few months previous, at the West Sixty-seventh Street apartment. His guests were having a good time and, in a mellow mood, Rip called Doug Storer aside.

"How about you and Hazel going back to China with me?" Ripley asked casually.

Storer protested that there was work to be done, the show had to go on, programs had been booked.

"Look," said Rip with a sudden urgency, "it won't be long before the Reds gobble up the rest of the country, gobble it up and close it up. This probably will be our last chance to go back."

The Storers were willing to return to China, but Doug insisted that he be given some time to work out a plan whereby he could combine business with pleasure. He remembered having read an advertisement in that morning's New York *Times* that a new flagship of the U. S. President Lines, the S.S. *President Cleveland,* was being commissioned to make its maiden voyage to the Orient in a few months.

The plan Storer worked out was to have Ripley and his entourage embark on that voyage, with Ripley using the steamship as a studio while doing his broadcasts for the National Broadcasting Company. The inducement for the U. S. President Lines was widespread publicity.

The night before the ship was to leave San Francisco, in April of 1948, Storer arranged for Ripley to make a guest appearance in Los Angeles on Ralph Edwards' "Truth or Consequences" show. One of the contestants was an ex-G.I., George McMillen, an incorrigible Dodger fan. His consequence if he failed was to get fifty coolies in Hong Kong to sign a petition declaring that the Dodgers' Leo Durocher was the greatest baseball manager in the world!

Physicians were waiting in the wings to give McMillen his inoculation shots when, inevitably, he failed. So George boarded the *President Cleveland.* (His trunk never did. The Golden Gate was far behind when the loss was discovered, and he had to be outfitted from the shop aboard ship and with clothes borrowed from other members of the party.)

There were five in the original Ripley party: Bob, Doug and Hazel Storer, Eddie Dunham, the NBC director of the Ripley show, and a secretary. McMillen made it six, and a seventh was added at Honolulu, when Li Ling Ai, the Chinese writer and lecturer, joined the party.

Storer, who was to have his headaches during the trip, had them during its preparation as well. Setting up the various programs to be short-waved back to the States took considerable doing, since plans had to be completed well in advance and at long range. It was one thing to arrange for McMillen to be on the "Truth or Consequences" show and another to be sure that there would be fifty coolies on hand in Hong Kong to sign the Durocher petition. The petition didn't help Leo, who was fired as Dodger manager in mid-season. Branch Rickey, then Brooklyn's resident genius, couldn't read Chinese.

While Doug was going furiously ahead with his preparations, he received a call from Ripley. "I'm not going on the trip," said Bob flatly. "I'm too tired. Call it off."

Storer dropped everything and raced up to see Ripley. Bob was tired, as he had said, but that wasn't the real reason for calling off the trip. He had asked a blond friend to go along and now he didn't want her to make the trip.

"Let's just say the trip is off, Doug," said Rip, "but don't call it off. Go right ahead quietly with all the plans and then, at the last minute, we'll go through with it. By that time it will be too late for her to get her shots, and we'll go without her."

Storer pleaded with Ripley. He tried to make the artist see that the entire success of the trip depended on advance publicity for the junket.

"Then it's off for good," said Rip and stormed from the room.

For the next few days the trip was off and on, with Ripley enthusiastic and moodish by turn. Storer continued to make plans as if there were no doubt about the tour; while Ripley kept telling his blond friend that the trip was definitely, absolutely, and positively off.

"If Storer's still planning on it, he's crazier than I thought he was!" yelled Rip.

When the S.S. *President Cleveland* steamed out of the Golden Gate, there was no blond friend aboard. But Ripley holed up in his cabin all the way from San Francisco to Honolulu, refusing to see anyone, refusing to look at any of the scripts prepared for him. He could have been sick. He certainly was "on the sauce." When the ship docked at Honolulu, Bob refused to grant an interview to the waiting newsmen.

Eventually Storer got Ripley on deck to grant a mass interview. Doug was pleased to have Ripley on his feet, for the broadcast planned there was an important one—the outcome of a contest run by the Honolulu paper which carried Rip's cartoon and which was published by an old friend, Riley Allen.

On this program Ripley also featured Li Ling Ai's mother. Both parents were highly respected doctors, the first Chinese to practice on the islands. Ling's mother, Dr. Li, had delivered more babies than any other doctor in the islands.

The show, and his meeting with the parents of his friend, temporarily elated Ripley. So did the discovery that Rudolf Friml was aboard, just as he had been on the 1932 trip to China. But Ripley retreated to his stateroom again as the ship headed for Manila. The lavish veranda room was in terrible disarray, littered with soiled clothes, unwashed glasses, the remains of meals, fruit peelings, shaving articles, stacked chairs, and rumpled bed clothing. The fact that Rip didn't bother to open his windows did nothing to make the quarters more inviting. He was morose, sullen, uncommunicative, and unapproachable.

Somehow he roused himself from his apathy to remember a promise he had made back in the States, to a Captain Wiest, who had been commandant of the Brooklyn Navy Yard. Wiest had lost a son early in World War II. The boy, taken prisoner by the Japanese, was on a transport bound for Japan when it was mistakenly bombed and sank with all hands.

When Ripley left on this trip, he obtained from Captain Wiest the exact latitude and longitude of the sunken ship. He also secured the co-operation of Captain Ehman of the *President Cleveland* for his plan. He had crew members make up a wreath. Late one sunny morning the big ship jogged a little from her course and, reversing her engines, slowed to a noiseless glide. When it reached the spot where so many young Americans had perished, Ripley picked up the wreath and cast it out on the gleaming water.

By one of those curious coincidences which seemed to fol-
low Ripley, there was another passenger aboard who had lost
a loved one—his brother—on the same Japanese transport, and
he too had a wreath to drop over the spot. He also arranged
with a clergyman, returning to his church in the Philippines,
to offer a prayer. The ship's engines had ceased their throb-
bing and there could be heard only the voice of the priest in-
toning the prayer for the dead.

This, again, was the paradoxical Ripley, softly and gently
sentimental after a period of sullen silence. Sudden change-
overs like this were startling, but rarely of any permanence,
and this somber phenomenon was more apparent in his last
few years.

At Manila, Ripley perked up again, doing tapes for a broadcast from the labyrinth of underground tunnels at Corregidor,
unmindful of the fact that they had not been completely
cleared of mines and booby traps planted by the Japanese.
There was no one on the island but a small detonation squad
under a young Filipino lieutenant. Only two or three weeks
before Ripley's visit another squad of about twenty-five men
had been wiped out by a mine in the Malinta Tunnel, which
had housed General Wainwright and his beleaguered forces.
Rip seemed exhilarated by the prospect or presence of danger,
showing more animation than he had since the party left San
Francisco. But that too passed, partly because of what he
found in Shanghai.

All the glory that had been Shanghai was gone by 1948.
The long exhausting years of war, the Japanese occupation,
the change in governments, the inexorable advance of the
Communists—all had taken their toll of the city which had
once been the First Lady of the Orient. For Rip it was like
meeting, after many years, an old flame who had become
soiled and shabby with age, illness, and misfortune.

Ripley saw all this, and perhaps, in it, a reflection of himself. He knew he would never see China again, that the China he was seeing now was not the China of his youth, any more than he was the dashing cartoonist who had taken New York and the nation by storm. It added to the deep, blue depression which was engulfing him.

At Hiroshima, Ripley interviewed survivors of the A bomb dropped by the *Enola Gay,* and in Tokyo he used the same studio from which Tokyo Rose had broadcast Japanese propaganda during World War II. He made the final leg of the trip by auto from Hiroshima to Yokohama to catch the *President Cleveland* back to Hawaii and the States. Most of the way he was a morose recluse.

Back home, the mood of depression which had swept over him was pierced by only occasional flashes of life and gaiety and satisfaction.

In his apartment he installed a huge Chinese lantern made of diminishing and descending circles of tiny dangling glass prisms decorated in many colors. It was like a delicate, shimmering cascade from the ceiling, and in the faintest stir of air the tiny prisms would sway and tinkle. For all its delicacy of design, the lantern was quite heavy, and hanging it in the high-ceiling section of the living room presented something of a problem in engineering. The ceiling had to be reinforced to bear its weight.

Ripley had picked up the chandelier-like ornament in Honolulu. It was characteristic of Bob that when the crate arrived, he couldn't wait to get the lantern hung, and while the workmen were buttressing the ceiling, Rip followed their every move. But after he had proudly exhibited the lantern at a couple of parties, the novelty wore off, and he was bored when a guest or visitor became enthusiastic about it.

Of a more serious concern to those who had known Bob

earlier was his growing intolerance of women. Although he
had been sporadically impatient with them, he now became
fed up with the wholesale female ménage of which he was
the hub and magnet. He tried to discard them, singly and
collectively, but it wasn't easy to demolish his auxiliary. He
resorted to insults and scenes. The women, however, were not
easily discouraged. Most of them felt they had earned "hash
marks" for their services under the Ripley flag and were determined to hang on to the bitter end, regardless of how
bitter it might become. Some stayed because it was a living;
some stayed because they loved him.

Ripley, for the first time, was becoming sensitive to jokes
about his multiple standard. Because so many of his entourage
and guests were Oriental, he found himself needled about his
role as "our unofficial ambassador to China." Once he had
laughed off such remarks; now he was genuinely irritated by
them.

At a Saints and Sinners luncheon in New York, at which
Ripley was the honored guest—or "fall guy"—Wellington Koo,
the Ambassador from China, was introduced on the dais and
asked if he might pose a question. Permission was granted.

"Mr. Ripley," he asked, "is it true what they say about
American women?"

The Saints and Sinners, being a little bit of each, roared at
Koo's question, and Rip joined in the general laughter. But
that was the exception, in those days.

Disturbed both physically and emotionally, Ripley was
given to more and more ugly scenes. He reached the point
where he was almost constantly disputatious, as if casting
about to become involved in arguments with friends and with
strangers. The shy man was now shouting—even screaming—
in public. Headwaiters trembled when they saw him approach
their velvet rope. No longer was Bob regarded as a high-

spending customer, but as a potential powder keg. Nobody knew what would set him off.

There was, in fact, something of a pattern in these rages. He would nag until his companion would give him the opening he was looking for. It might be no more than a mild, "Oh, come now, Bob. You know that's not so," which would serve as the fuse.

"You're calling me a liar!" he would roar, and then he'd be off.

The unusual thing about Ripley's blowups was that he contrived to have most of those in earshot believe that he was in the right, that he had been wronged and was shouting only in self-defense.

Victims of these Ripley tirades vowed that Bob would never get another opportunity to lash at them, but the next day, or shortly thereafter, he would be on the telephone, full of contrition and apologies. "I don't know what's coming over me" was his favorite defense.

"I had heard about these blowups of Roy's and even witnessed one or two," Vyvyan Donner, his long-time friend, recalled. "He seemed pretty much the same to me, even though I knew he was drinking a great deal more than he had before.

"One night I was the victim of one of his explosions. While he had been going into these dreadful fits of temper for years, he had always passed me up. I thought it was because we had been such good friends—we'd always called each other for advice before taking any new step; for instance, Roy asked me my opinion of making movie shorts, and I asked him when I was offered the job of fashion editor for Fox Movietonews. But this particular evening I learned Roy didn't care who he shouted at."

Ripley telephoned Miss Donner and asked her out to dinner. They hadn't seen each other in so long, he said, and he was losing touch with so many of his friends.

"I accepted because I was genuinely fond of Roy and had found his company stimulating," she explained.

At the appointed time, Ripley called for Miss Donner in his chauffeur-driven car. When they were settled in the car, Bob asked her where they should dine.

"Anyplace you like," replied Miss Donner.

"No, you name it," Ripley insisted. "You've let me make the choice too often."

"Well, you've been the host, and I always thought you should select the place. Would you like some French food?"

"Whatever you say; you're calling the shots."

"Or maybe you'd like Italian food?"

"You name it and we'll go there."

Miss Donner realized she'd either have to select a restaurant or both would starve to death in the back seat of Ripley's limousine.

"All right," said Miss Donner resignedly, "let's go to the Penthouse."

"The Penthouse!" Ripley screamed, as if the word stabbed him. "You must be getting goofy. How could you suggest going to a dump like that? The food's lousy and you know it. You want to see me poisoned? Is that your idea? Is that what you want?"

Like so many of Ripley's previous targets, Miss Donner was trapped. She couldn't very well leap out of Ripley's car while the tirade was spending itself. She tried to mollify Rip.

"I only mentioned the Penthouse because you insisted I name the place," she said quietly. "I don't care where we go to dinner. Take me anyplace you'd care to go."

"You said the Penthouse and that's where we're going," said Ripley stubbornly. At that he switched moods and went into his I-don't-know-what's-come-over-me routine. Miss

Donner thought she had managed to ride out the storm. When they arrived at the Penthouse and entered the elevator to go to the eleventh-floor dining room, Ripley began his scathing criticism of the restaurant all over again, in a loud and angry voice. Miss Donner looked straight ahead, but Ripley wasn't letting her off easily.

"And you," he yelled, leveling a finger at her, "you suggested this dump! You picked it out!"

After the headwaiter had seated them, Ripley erupted again. Addressing the headwaiter imperiously, he demanded that they be moved to a table on the other side of the room. What sort of knucklehead did the *maître d'* think he, Ripley, was, to be placed on that side of the lousy dining room?

"What could you do?" Miss Donner asked as she related the harrowing experience. "Flounce out of the restaurant? He had you trapped, and he seemed to take a sadistic pleasure in the terrible embarrassment. There was no possibility of your enjoying the dinner after a scene like that. Then he quieted down, suddenly, became apologetic and said he must be sick to act as he had. I accepted his apologies and made a mental vow never to go with him alone again, never to allow myself to be placed in a position where he could humiliate me."

It was not only Ripley's dinner guests who were finding him difficult. Crystal Waters, a diction teacher who had tutored Rip in his speech for his radio shows and had effected a great improvement in his delivery, was another victim. She found Ripley an earnest pupil, except for those occasions when he flew into blind rages and asked her who had ever told her she was a speech teacher.

When one series of Miss Waters' lessons ended, Ripley received quite a number of compliments on his improved technique. Bob figured that if one series had made such an improvement, a second series might work wonders. Miss Waters was invited back for another tutoring job. The pay, substantial for the first course, was to be even better. Miss Waters turned this down.

"I just couldn't go through that again," she said with a shudder.

The once dapper artist was becoming increasingly careless about his personal appearance. More than once he received guests unshaven, with a pepper-and-salt stubble on his chin.

Often he would leave Bion clad only in his sleazy bathrobe and a pair of Oriental slippers and ride in his chauffeured car to his West Side apartment.

Rip also displayed indifference to public opinion by his querulousness with interviewers. Bob was, of course, excellent source material for the fan magazines. Storer tried to set up most of the fan-magazine interviews for Bion. It was good showmanship, for Bion, crammed with oddities from the four corners of the earth, made an admirable background. But it didn't make for a good press when a writer had made the trek from Midtown Manhattan to Mamaroneck only to find that Ripley wasn't receiving that day.

When Ripley did consent to an interview, he was affable and gracious—at the start, at least. He would have Mrs. Doud, his housekeeper, or one of the ladies in residence, show the visitor about his studio. He would answer questions modestly.

In the second stage of the interview, Ripley would grow listless, then restless. He would excuse himself frequently, perhaps to tipple. Sometimes he wouldn't return after one of his exits and one of the women would take over, explaining that Mr. Ripley had a long-distance call or a headache and were there any questions she could answer, anything on which the interviewer needed to be filled in?

Whether Ripley remained for the end of the interview or

whether a female stand-in tied up the loose ends, it always was concluded with a Ripleyesque gesture—the interviewer was given a coach ticket from Mamaroneck to Grand Central Station on the New York, New Haven & Hartford. The income of a free-lancer for a fan magazine being what it was, this gesture sent the writer away with a good impression of the subject.

If Rip gave interviewers something less than the full attention they wanted, they were not alone in their difficulty. Ripley often seemed preoccupied. He spent a good deal of time, for example, drawing plans for a hospital room he was going to endow in Oakie's name. It was to be for sufferers of cancer —which had claimed Oakie—and the emphasis was on creating a mood of lightness and joy for the beholder, with gay colors and furnishings. He never finished his plans.

Playing host could, to the end, at least temporarily shake Ripley out of his black moods. Even after the rather unhappy China visit, Rip put on two huge dinner parties at his Manhattan apartment, at which he lavished Oriental hospitality, announced facts about the fare, and seemed to enjoy everything.

Ostensibly the dinners were to permit friends such as Eddie Rickenbacker, president of Eastern Air Lines, to see a private viewing of the J. Arthur Rank films of the 1948 Olympics, which had been held that summer in London. Actually Rip simply wanted an excuse to preside over a formal Chinese dinner once more. Rip's enthusiasm in asking his friends to ask *their* friends resulted in such a raft of acceptances that he had to hold two dinner parties on successive nights to accommodate everybody.

Bob spent the winter of 1948–49 more or less happily at Hi-Mount. After New Year's, Rip had as house guests there a couple of whom he was extremely fond, Jim and Marjorie

Young, whom he had met in Shanghai in 1932. Young was at that time working on the Japan *Advertiser* and finally went to a Japanese concentration camp after the Sino-Japanese war erupted into a global conflict.

It was a joyous reunion when Ripley was able to catch up with the Youngs after Jimmy had been released from concentration camp and reunited with his wife. Bob helped them get started again in the newspaper business in this country, and Jimmy was with the Anderson, South Carolina, *Daily Mail*.

Ripley was supremely happy with the Youngs, and he and Jim made plans for the golden anniversary of the *Daily Mail*. Bob and Young got together on a promotion stunt, in conjunction with the annual meeting of the South Carolina Junior Chamber of Commerce. The *Daily Mail* was to conduct a statewide "Believe It or Not" contest. Bob was to arrive in his junk outside Charleston and then be driven to Columbia and to Anderson for a special "Believe It or Not" celebration. Rip was to judge the contest and award prizes.

Ripley's old enthusiasm for projects of this sort returned full blast. He assembled a small album of "Believe It or Not" cartoons pertaining to South Carolina, including one revealing that the statue to the Confederate War dead erected by the United Daughters of the Confederacy in Court House Park, Bennettsville, South Carolina, in 1907 was that of a Union soldier. The Italian sculptor had made the mistake.

Young's *Daily Mail*, in its fiftieth-anniversary number in 1949, contained on its cover page more than a half-dozen Ripley cartoons pertaining to the Palmetto State, plus a somber news story that the cartoonist had died of a heart attack in New York a few days before he was to leave for South Carolina.

Hectic is a hapless word for Rip's last days. The last romantic flame was a Cuban girl who was moved into Hi-Mount, while the other girls sniffed, without a word of warning. Ripley had several stories about how he had met her. They never agreed. But there was no question about her being the harem favorite: Rip began taking her for rides on a tandem bicycle he treasured.

They made an interesting pair on their cycling trips along Lake Worth. Rip's idea of proper cycling attire was somewhat warped. He affected a wild Gay Nineties checkered cap, a false policeman's mustache from the same era, and long red flannel drawers. The Cuban girl just wore tight red drawers. They pedaled sedately through the long lazy days, followed by most of the children and possibly all of the dogs in Palm Beach.

A blonde broke up that last-ditch stand. The Cuban girl imported her as a "companion." There was always room for another girl in Rip's house. With a burst of hospitality, he turned his big bedroom over to the two girls on their first night together and slept in his den. Or, at least, he tried to sleep. The house shook with their giggles through the night.

The blonde brought along a puppy who was declared ill, by Ripley, on the second day of her visit. He asked her to take the dog to a vet, but she refused. The dog died the following day, and a great storm began brewing in Ripley. He began to drink in earnest.

To complicate matters, it was the cook's night off, and the girls, in an excess of ambition—or maybe thinking to propitiate Ripley—offered to make the dinner. The Youngs and Storers retreated upstairs to dress, and the noise of slamming pots and pans and high giggles from the kitchen could be heard in the upper reaches of the house. Then, suddenly, there was silence.

Hazel Storer happened to be the first one downstairs. She

saw Bob in the dining room, seated at the end of the long, dark, polished table. The room was dimly lit by candles. Ripley sat motionless, holding his head in those large athlete's hands, a look of black fury on his face. The flickering light of the candles in the dark room made the scene more ominous. Alarmed, Hazel went over to Rip, dropped an arm soothingly on his shoulder, and asked what the trouble was.

He burst out into a long, not-too-coherent tirade about the girls. It was so mixed up that it made little sense. Hazel left him and went into the kitchen, where she found the two girls standing in the middle of the room, clinging to each other in sheer panic. Bob, brooding over the treatment of the puppy and the casual approach to the preparation of the dinner, had stormed into the kitchen, threatening the girls with physical harm.

A contributing factor to Ripley's black moods was his discovery, a few days before the Storers and Youngs arrived for this Hi-Mount visit, that his personal account was $17,000 short. It wasn't a mystery, either. One of his girl friends, whom he had entrusted with some of his nonbusiness financial affairs, had done some rather inept juggling of his checkbook, to her own enrichment. His accountant had been down from New York and advised Ripley to fire the girl. Furious as he was, Rip couldn't bring himself to fire her. He compromised by banishing her temporarily from the inner circle.

And, fortunately for her, Rip's attention was drawn away from this financial loss by a couple of other losses more important to him. During that winter, Virtue, one of his prize spaniels, fell through the ice at Bion and drowned. Rip was almost beside himself. Fond as he was of animals, he mourned its passing as he would a human's departure from this vale.

Shortly after he returned to New York from Hi-Mount, Rip had the Storers over for dinner, to commiserate. Shanghai had fallen to the Communists. Rip took Hazel by the hand as soon as she and Doug got off the elevator and led her into his big, gloomy bedroom. He sat down on the bed and cried.

"We'll never see China again," he said over and over again, the tears streaming down his face.

There are those among his friends who believe that the loss of China to the Communists—who represented the ultimate evil to him—was a factor in Rip's death. Indeed he felt it deeply, for his identification with this faraway land was nearly total. He was in love with it. At any rate, he now found it difficult to work up enthusiasm about much of anything, although he continued to carry a load of work which was increased by the start of a TV series for the Motorola Company.

It was a short but eventful life in television for Ripley. The series, which was in effect a visual interpretation of his old radio show, got under way on March 1, 1949, and featured one of the stars from his radio past, Kuda Bux. This time the fakir's task was somewhat less harrowing. Instead of walking on a bed of glowing coals, he would attempt to ride blindfolded through several laps of a six-day bike race then grinding away at an uptown New York armory.

I was the "remote" man on that initial Ripley telecast. through my earphones I could hear him, his voice rising excitedly from his downtown studio, ordering me to get Kuda Bux on the road. I saw the hot little red eye of the TV camera at the armory glow on. I attended to tying the cloth around Kuda Bux's head, at eye level, and was afraid I'd hurt him. The man kept saying, "Tighter . . . tighter." I made it tight.

"Now, there he goes!" I could hear Ripley shouting—downtown. I helped Kuda Bux on a bike, steadied him briefly, and launched him on his way around the steeply banked wooden oval.

He made it fine, the first lap, but that must have emboldened him, for he tried a second lap—with the camera still on him. Almost made it too. But just as he came in for a triumphant closeup, he lost control of his bike and went flat on his face. Blood streamed from his nose, but he brushed a blob of it away as if it were nothing and took his bow. Ripley's TV career was off to a characteristically eccentric start.

(Actually, Rip had had a go at the medium when it was in an experimental stage. He did three programs for NBC in 1941 —when there were only thirty-five hundred sets in New York, and a handful outside the city—and won top rating in the primitive type of Nielsen then in use: NBC polled the set owners by postcard. The demands of World War II cut TV off in its infancy, and thereby postponed the flowering of Ripley on television.)

The Ripley TV show might be described as a "Believe It or Not" variety show, including interviews with people who had done something highly unusual or lived through a strange experience; dramatizations of the Ripley type of odd or arresting occurrence; cartooning by Ripley; and displays of curious objects Rip had collected around the world. The commercials, incidentally, were done by two Chinese comedians, Ming and Ling: in one, they portrayed characters who did not want to leave a burning building because Ripley was on TV; in another, they were picked up by an Irish cop for speeding on their way to the studio providing an opportunity for an interplay of accents.

For a variety of reasons the most notable of Bob's thirteen TV shows were numbers twelve and thirteen. On Number Twelve, there was a solid human-interest dramatization of how a young choirboy was forced to defend himself against neighborhood toughs, and grew up to be the great light-heavyweight boxing champ, Tommy Loughran. That show also featured a Ripley interview with Bill Corum, the late great sports writer, sportscaster and, for a time, head man of the Kentucky Derby. The occasion for Bill's appearance was the incredible forecast he had made of the 1949 Derby. Bill correctly picked the first four horses in order: Ponder, Capot, Palestinian, and Old Rockport, and you'd have to get into the realm of higher mathematics to figure the odds on a prediction like that being borne out. The prepared q. and a. for the interview missed, by a couple of lengths, capturing the flavor of Corum's speech. But if the show introduced Bill to even a few people who might otherwise have never come in contact with the great man, it served a highly worthwhile purpose.

Ripley's last TV show was remarkable for a drama that was unscheduled and was played without the audience's being aware of it. The *pièce de résistance* was (ironically enough, as one would expect from Ripley) a dramatization of the origin of "Taps." The denouement of this is a coincidence incredible even by Rip's standards: a Union army captain crawls out of a trench at the sound of moaning coming from a wounded Confederate soldier; drags the boy back to safety under withering gunfire; discovers the boy is his own son; finds in his son's pockets a sheet of music which the boy had written and which is played over his grave, and which is, one hardly need add, "Taps." That was the customary "dramatic blackout."

There had been a blackout of another nature earlier in the show. Rip was displaying a collection of models of the crown jewels of Europe. The routine prepared for the show was to have Rip hold up various of the crowns and orbs and explain their significance to a lush redhead on the show, Peggy Corday. But Doug Storer had done some routining that Rip didn't know about. Because Rip was quite clearly a sick man—and had blacked out a few times in the preceding months—Storer took the precaution of running Peggy through a special rehearsal of the significance of the crowns. As had been feared by Storer, Rip blacked out completely under the hot video lights as he started to go through the crown part of the show. He was holding up a crown, and began to say, "And this, Peggy, is . . ." when he lost consciousness. Peggy took over, saying, "Yes, Bob, I know what that is; it's . . ." And, holding Bob up with a sisterly arm around his shoulder, she finished the act and helped him back to his chair without anyone in the audience the wiser.

Storer and other friends of Ripley had been telling him that he ought to get into a hospital for a thorough checkup. He had suffered from hypertension for some time. After this show, he sullenly turned to Storer and said, "All right, damn it, I'll do what you want, I'll go to the hospital." The show was on Tuesday, May 24. He entered Harkness Pavilion of the Columbia Presbyterian Medical Center on Thursday.

The end for Robert L. Ripley was sudden. He had been in the hospital for two days when, on the afternoon of May 27, he called Bugs Baer. "I'm just in for a checkup," he reassured his wonderful old friend, "and I'll be out to the farm to see you tomorrow." He put the telephone back in its cradle and buckled over on the pillow, dead of a heart attack.

The funeral service at St. James Protestant Episcopal Church on May 31 drew the kind of a crowd Rip was most at home with—Bugs Baer, Eddie Rickenbacker, Jack Dempsey, Howard Chandler Christy among the four hundred there. The body was shipped back to Santa Rosa, where the whole story had started, for burial.

Rip had written what amounted to his own epilogue a couple of years before his death. A painstaking search of his three homes and *Mon Lei* after his death turned up a will dated April 4, 1947, and written aboard the junk. After providing that the bulk of his million-dollar estate be left in trust to his sister, Mrs. Ethel Davis, and his estranged brother, Doug (who survived him by only a couple of years), Ripley turned to those who had figured prominently or dramatically in his life.

Carol Ennis, who propelled the stripling into his first job in San Francisco, was left $2500. Walter St. Denis, the alert editor who was at the very least instrumental in creating "Believe It or Not," got $1000. There also was $1000 each for Vyvyan Donner and Bugs Baer, both of whom had provided Rip with love and affection for some thirty-five years; $1000 for Bradley Kelly and for Ward Greene, who had succeeded Joe Connolly at KFS when Connolly died in 1945.

Bequests of $5000 went to some members of his staff—Norbert Pearlroth, his chief researcher, and William McDonald, a secretary. Another secretary got $5000, as did Jean Doud, the housekeeper at Bion. There was $5000 too for Douglas Storer, who had suffered untold agonies in getting and keeping Ripley in front of a microphone.

Most of these bequests were shockingly inadequate. But it is a mark of the largely inexplicable effect Ripley had on a great many people that those who had felt the urge to help him in his lifetime rushed forward with excuses for the harsh way he had treated them in death. None of them really pretended to explain Ripley fully, and almost all would, at one point or another in conversation about him, echo Joe Connolly in saying: "Ripley was his own greatest 'Believe It or Not.'"

Even now, mention of Ripley among friends or slight acquaintances can bring forth a flood of anecdotes (some, fact; more, fiction) about his life and career, and an uncommon amount of diverse speculation about what made him tick. In the post-mortems on Bob's personality there is remarkably little unanimity as to what had given him such a commanding hold on the attention of millions of people.

There *is* a consensus that what Rip achieved was indeed incredible: the poor, uneducated Ripley risen to the premier position among newspaper cartoonists; the unsophisticated Ripley roaming the world, becoming a twentieth-century Marco Polo; the inordinately shy, stammering Ripley overcoming the most oppressive case of mike fright on record to become one of the most successful of all radio-TV personalities.

It is something of a certainty too that on the fateful afternoon in 1918 when Bob couldn't muster enough material for his regular sports cartoon, he brought forth (with St. Denis's midwife-like assistance) one of the really magnetic and durable ideas of modern American journalism. "Believe It or Not" as an idea has endured long after Rip's death, and survived that death considerably better than his more worldly possessions.

Bion was purchased after Rip's death by Ferruccio Tagliavini, the opera singer. He kept it only a short while and sold the property to two men who demolished the mansion to make way for more modern housing. Although there certainly were people around with the means to maintain a place like Bion, there was no one who combined with money the kind of flamboyance inbred in Ripley that made Bion perfect for him.

The motley contents of Bion were scattered. Some of the *objets d'art* went at auction. The collection of steins brought $20,000 from a brewery, and is now valued at $100,000. Some things disappeared, including the display of erotica. The Palm Beach house was sold. *Mon Lei* passed through a succession of owners and into the hands of a New York and

Florida entrepreneur. A big feature spread on the junk in a magazine a dozen years after Rip's death did not even mention him as the former owner.

But a large number of "Believe It or Not" books have appeared since the originator's death—Storer brought out eight editions while he was president of the Believe It or Not Corporation, and more than 1,500,000 copies were sold. The "Believe It or Not" TV show continued for almost two years after the unlucky thirteenth program that was Rip's last.

Among the informal memorials to Ripley's idea is the continuing hobby of Wayne Harbour, a butter-and-egg man in Bedford, Iowa. Since November 1, 1943, Harbour has made a point of writing to every person, next of kin of same, or institution, or city, mentioned in the "Believe It or Not" newspaper cartoon. In a recent letter to Storer he submitted the following accounting: "I have written:—16,241 letters of inquiry, 7,231 replies received, 3,270 letters returned, and 5,740 remain unanswered."

Around the world, millions of people (more passive fans than Harbour) still are amazed, intrigued, or annoyed by newspaper versions of "Believe It or Not." And the perfect sign-off to any weird, outrageous, or merely apocryphal story remains:

Believe It or Not.